THE KAYAK LADY

One Woman · One Kayak · 1007 Lakes

10/4/10

Keep Paddling!

Mary

TKL

THE KAYAK LADY: One Woman, One Kayak, 1007 Lakes

ISBN: 978-0-578-04891-8

Cover photos by Derek Montgomery, *Duluth News Tribune*

Edited by Vicki Nelson

Book and cover design by Gilsvik Book Production

Map provided by Itasca County

Printed by Bang Printing

First Printing 2010

10 9 8 7 6 5 4 3 2 1

CHICKADEE
LAKE
PRESS

Contact Chickadee Lake Press for more information:

Chickadee Lake Press
1036 Northeast Third Avenue
Grand Rapids, MN 55744

www.marythekayaklady.com

To everyone who knows and loves the lakes of Itasca County,
with special thanks to all who supported and assisted me
in kayaking each of those 1,007 lakes

www.marythekayaklady.com

Mary Shideler is available for presentations and readings.
For information, visit marythekayaklady.com.

An orange cap, long sleeves, and pants tucked in tall boots …
but still losing the battle with insects on the long walk into Finley Lake.

Contents

oodwinked

Mother Nature often imitates herself. More than once I have mistaken a bright yellow goldfinch for a dandelion head. Other times I believed I was looking at the outstretched neck of a great blue heron when it was really the gray upturned roots of tipped over trees along the water's edge. Sticking out of the water for air, stubby snapping turtle heads resemble deadheads, while the pointy heads of painted turtles look like small sticks. From a distance, lily pad roots may appear to be ducks. Mother Nature is clever, and she has taught me to look carefully so that I may discern what is really there and what is not.

About the Lake Names

Lakes are named for a variety of reasons including shape, contents, surroundings, and people who may have lived nearby. Many lakes have descriptive or intriguing names like Buttonbox, Half Moon, or Nose. Some lake names reoccur. There are nine Bass Lakes, nine Long Lakes, eight Spring Lakes, and seven Moose Lakes in Itasca County, and at least two each of lakes named Deer, Pickerel, and Stumple.

To add to the confusion, some bodies of water are known by more than one name. An example is Rice Lake, described in "Rice Lake Floatplane," a chapter in this book. Some people are more likely to know that isolated body of water as Round Lake. An extreme case of multiple names is a lake in the northeast corner of the county that goes by Fox, Lemen, and Roebuck.

Readers who are sufficiently curious about unfamiliar names or locations can find the bodies of water included in this kayaking adventure on a good Itasca County map.

Lakes and Major Rivers in Itasca County, Minnesota

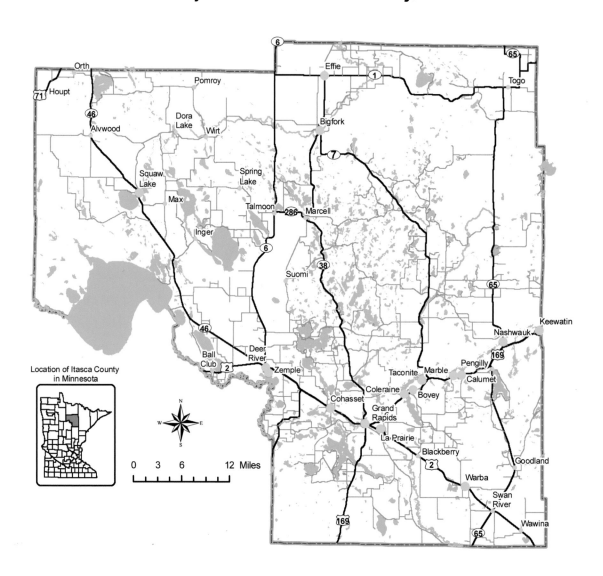

At one point there were 237 unnamed lakes in Itasca County. The Minnesota Department of Natural Resources (DNR) identified those lakes by number. In the summer of 2007, friends suggested I name a lake. After 11 months of effort, Itasca County Lake #628 officially became Chickadee Lake. It took a signed petition, the support of the Itasca County Board of Commissioners, the DNR, and the United States Board of Geographic Names to approve the new name. Chickadee Lake is typical of my favorites. It is a 23-acre, clear-water lake surrounded by stately pines and birch trees. Its only residents are nonhuman: beaver, deer, loons, and, of course, the perky black-capped chickadees that make Itasca County their year-round home.

Mary looks across an overgrown and abandoned beaver dam to find a route out of DNR Lake #310.

From Back O' the Moon

Lured to the mystery of woods and water at an early age, it is little wonder that I developed a passion to kayak all of the lakes in Itasca County. Being fifty percent Russian and one hundred percent curious did not hurt either.

My family owned Back O' the Moon Resort on Bass Lake, a short drive from Grand Rapids, Minnesota. Seven housekeeping cabins, each with a wood-burning fireplace, sat along a charming cove named Wolf Bay. We rented by the week to people who came from the Minneapolis-Saint Paul area or as far away as Iowa, Illinois, Indiana, Ohio, and beyond. A few times we had guests from overseas who did not speak English. I did my best to make friends with everyone. In return, I learned about diversity and had ample opportunity to see how other people lived—at least how they lived while on vacation. Often I was invited to eat dinner in a guest's cabin, to go fishing, or to join a family on a hike. A few lifelong friendships developed with our return guests. I even adopted a set of grandparents, and I am thankful they adopted me back.

Although there was a 40-year span between us, my parents included me in most of their favorite pastimes. Behind the resort, our wooded 40 acres adjoined county land where we had brushed out cross-country ski trails. While Dad and I were skiing back there one winter afternoon, he taught me to look at the snow with care and to study the dull gray hairs that a deer had left behind when it passed by. On that same acreage, I occasionally joined Dad for grouse and deer hunting. He would often fall asleep in the leaf litter while I quietly sat with my back leaning against a sturdy oak. My mind gently wandered as I imagined shapes in the clouds passing overhead and considered just how Mother Nature kept track of so many different things.

Dad also took Mom and me fishing. On calm June evenings we used one of the 14-foot aluminum resort boats to putt-putt out to a sunken island to fish for walleyes; later in the summer we took the old speedboat a few miles down the lake to the bullhead hole. Winter fishing was a different kind of venture. The chainsaw and I shared a sled that Dad towed onto the ice behind the snowmobile. When we arrived at a good fishing spot, Dad would start the saw and shout, "Stand back, Pal!"

Once the saw was revved up, ice chips flew, and we soon had a hole in the ice and a place to put our fish house.

For many years my folks bought season tickets to downhill ski at one of the local ski resorts. Mom gave me an early start when she strapped my three-year-old feet to a pair of old wooden skis and sent me down the small slope in front of the chalet. When the driveway into the resort became smooth and icy, we took advantage of the situation by bringing out our old runner sled. We all enjoyed wild rides as we tried to make the corner at the bottom of the hill.

One clear and frigid January evening, we bundled up and marched onto the frozen lake with binoculars in hand to find the comet Kohoutek. Dad had read about the comet in *Time* and decided we were going to see it for ourselves. Kohoutek was not as bright as scientists had predicted, but we saw it.

On another winter evening, my parents, our neighbors, and I were skating on a small area we had cleared on the lake in front of the resort. A brilliant full moon lit our way as we did homemade tricks on the ice and played tag. At one point, Dad called out to me, "Pal, come on over here so I can show you something."

I made my way over to the shoreline in front of cabin number five. Dad pointed at the bank and said, "Look at the shadow the moon has cast from these wild rose bushes."

And look I did. Time froze. There, lightly traced in the snow, perfect and frail, were the thin, subtle gray branches of the wild rose bushes. That moment remains etched in my memory.

For a number of summers my brother Bob, 12 years my senior, and I would attempt to water ski together sharing just one ski while Dad had the old speedboat coughing and smoking at full throttle. Bob positioned his feet in the bindings and had his hands locked onto the towrope while I clamped my arms around his waist and hung on for all I was worth. When and if we ever got organized enough to stay up, I would wedge my feet against Bob's. Once I had to just let go for no good reason other than the bottom of my bikini had been ripped off from the spray of the ski. We had big fun.

> "Pal, come on over here so I can show you something."
> – Dad

When I was in middle school, a resort guest named David brought his Sunfish sailboat to the resort. David taught me to sail, and a year later I bought a 14-foot sailboat with my own earnings. One gusty spring afternoon, I turtled the boat while taking my neighbor for a ride. A trio of young men was watching from shore. They immediately roared out in their small speedboat, cut the motor, and dove in to help flip the boat upright. I became a better sailor after that.

Life at the resort was not always that active. Quieter activities taught me to be resourceful. In late July Mom and I would go raspberry and blueberry picking. I would be nervously looking around for bears that never materialized. Usually I quit picking after a laborious 20 minutes and hoped that the single layer of blueberries on the bottom of my ice cream bucket would be enough to make muffins.

All of those experiences helped define who I grew to be, but my yen for adventure received a real boost one afternoon when I was a chatty five-year-old. A memorable resort guest named Val came over to converse while I played on the swing set. Val was an English professor. She was attractive and very physically fit. Also kind, she gave me plenty of attention. I liked to play on the swing set as it was close to her cabin. I could appear to be busy swinging when really I was staring at Val's cabin door waiting for her to come out to play. On that day, Val and I were discussing Native Americans. She informed me that she was an Indian.

"How can that be?" I challenged with disbelief in my voice. "You have blond hair and blue eyes."

Undaunted, Val simply explained, "If you paddle your canoe through the reeds, you are indeed a real Indian."

From that moment on, I intended to become a real Indian living on the shores of Big Bass Lake. Val woke my passion to explore lakes and streams.

Traveling both the paved roads and the gravel byways of Itasca County, I passed by many lakes over the years. In doing so I often considered what a lake was really like beyond what could be seen from the road, how soft the bottom of a creek was, or how large an island might be. By the time I was 30 years old, I realized I had actually only been on, or in, about a half dozen area lakes. Always looking for an adventure, I decided a kayak was my boat of choice. Still married at the time, I convinced my husband Gary to build one for me.

Gary and I had taken many canoe trips to the Quetico and Boundary Waters. We often went with a friend who traveled by kayak. The efficiency of the kayak intrigued me. It cut smoothly through the water, and, unlike the canoe, it was not tossed around by the wind. The idea that a person could paddle alone was very appealing to me.

I wanted a kayak that would happily accommodate my four-foot nine-inch, 94-pound frame. I pictured a boat that tracked straight on the water, was durable yet lightweight enough for me to lift and carry alone. After a winter of research, I ordered a kayak kit from Pygmy Boats in the spring of 1996. A few weeks later UPS delivered two brown boxes that I opened and immediately emptied. The long box contained mahogany plywood strips; the heavy square box held epoxy and fiberglass cloth construction materials. Having never worked with a kit before, and possessing minimal spatial reasoning skills, I could not envision a completed kayak taking form from the assorted articles spread out on the garage floor.

Gary, on the other hand, knew exactly what to do and where to begin. Carefully following the step-by-step instructions, he stitched the panels together using small wire twists. Then he glued the seams with epoxy, removed the wires, and applied fiberglass. After weeks of labor—a total of 102 active hours—the sleek 13-foot long, 22-inch wide, 32-pound kayak was ready for a float test.

Although the sun was about to kiss the horizon, we loaded the little kayak inside our van—where it fit with a quarter inch to spare—and rushed down to Ice Lake, just a block from our home. With the care of a new mother, I gently placed the little beauty into the water. I was excited and nervous. At the same time I was filled with anticipation as I took the first strong strokes away from shore. Gary cheered, and so did I. An onlooker applauded. There were no leaks. All of the time and effort put into making and keeping the keel straight paid off as my kayak tracked perfectly.

My dream of owning a kayak had come true. Little did I know that dream would develop into an obsession to kayak every one of Itasca County's lakes.

Mary prepares to take a water clarity reading as she lowers her Secchi disk into Ice Lake.

In the beginning I learned there were 1,007 lakes in the county. As time went on, I questioned the exact number of lakes as my county lake listing only numbered to 945. Eleven years into the project, as I was approaching that magical 945 number, I began to wonder where the phantom 62 lakes were. Thinking they might be mine pits, I checked with the Department of Natural Resources (DNR), the Itasca County Assessor's Office, and the Itasca County Soil and Water Conservation District. "No," I was told, "mine pits did not make up the missing 62 lakes."

In the old days, the DNR defined a lake in Minnesota as a body of water of 10 acres or more. With the exception of a handful of lakes, including Miller Lake that dried up after a beaver dam burst, the number of lakes in the county remained the same. It was the definition of a lake that had changed, resulting in numbers ranging from 940 to 1,075. I decided to paddle the 945 lakes on my original lake list and find 62 other bodies of water that met the DNR's new definition to qualify as a lake.

These are the DNR criteria I used. A body of water met the requirements to be called a lake if 1) it was five or more feet deep, 2) it had a windswept shoreline, or 3) it was a body of water of a "sizeable" size—my personal favorite, just because it sounded

like pure government doublespeak to me.

Since I took water clarity readings with a dinner-plate-sized Secchi disk on a calibrated rope, it was easy to determine water depth. I just lowered the disk over the side of the kayak until the rope went slack, indicating that the disk had hit bottom. Then I pulled the disk back up and simply counted the feet of wet rope. The last Secchi disk I was given came with 29 feet of rope. As my boyfriend, Horsethief Harry Johnson, observed in his wise way, the computer used to process lake depth information must have only been able to count up to 29. Of course many lakes were well over 29 feet deep. My first well-worn Secchi disk was attached to a 44-foot rope that sometimes was not long enough to hit the bottom of a lake either.

Water clarity and depth data were passed along to the Itasca County Soil and Water Conservation District and to the Minnesota Pollution Control Agency. One year, the *Report on the Transparency of Minnesota Lakes* by the Citizen Lake-Monitoring Program stated that Itasca County had more lakes monitored than any other county in the state due to one woman with a kayak.

Launching the kayak into Ice Lake that long ago evening changed my life. From then on I had my ticket to getting acquainted with and unlocking secrets of the county's lakes, bogs, and creeks. My kayaking adventures were underway.

Westward Ho

The sun is in the wrong position. I know for sure I am not facing west. But how can the sun be wrong? Well, it is. I know my compass is off too. And this topographic map is so old it must be outdated. Hmmm. This creek is a great deal longer than it looks on the map. At least I am paddling with the current. Good, here is the lake. Hey! Wait a minute. That little island looks familiar. Why, this is Gunn Lake, not Charlie Lake! I must have launched on Charlie Lake instead of Blind Lake! Who is the blind one here? Please accept my apologies sun, compass, and topo map. My mistake, not yours. Whoops!

A tiny spring peeper contemplates a big world.

Dragonfly Magic

Like most three-year-olds, I believed in mother magic. If Mom said it was so, I just went along with it. Growing up on the lake at the resort offered ample opportunity to ask Mom many questions. One fond memory was the day I discovered the little dead dragons hanging on the cabin's foundation. When I asked about them, Mom told me they were the left-behind skins dragonflies wore when they lived in the water. I never thought too much about how or why a dragonfly could, or even would, be able to live in those little crusty casings that were about the size of my thumb. I just accepted it and knew that some smart grown-up scientist who studied bugs would know the details. That was good enough for me.

When I was a little older and allowed to explore closer to the water, I often found the fragile gray-tan shells clinging to a dock post or tree trunk. Moving slowly and carefully, I would pick the hulls from their resting places and give them an extensive examination. I was always mindful not to crush the treasures. No dragonfly had ever hurt me, and I knew dragonflies were helpful. They lived up to their "mosquito hawk" nickname by eating many of the tiny insects each day. From an early age, I had reverence for the dragonfly.

Once a resort guest teasingly mentioned that dragonflies were just sewing machine needles with wings. If I talked too much, he said, one would come along and sew my lips shut. For a long time after that, I really wondered if there was any truth behind people referring to dragonflies as darning needles. Less daring resort guests had strong concerns regarding the ugly and frightening monster-look-alike things hanging on their cabins. They even asked if we could please remove them. I thought those people were not very brave or nice. I wondered how they could ever take fish off their own hooks and why they were vacationing in the north woods if they did not get along with insects.

In school we learned about the transition a dragonfly makes from aquatic larva to adult. Conditions have to be just right for such a wonder to occur. Depending on the type of dragonfly, that moment might be any time from a few months to a few years, but they are equipped to wait it out. When it is time, the larvae leave their water habitat and usually climb onto a vertical surface to transform into adults. Apparently, they have no uncomfortable teenage years in which they experience pimples, being grounded, or needing to borrow the car. They magically shift from propelling underwater in prehistoric swim togs to obtaining form-fitting flight suits and pilots' licenses in about an hour's time. Adult dragonflies live a fast life whether they want to or not. By the end of summer, nearly all will be dead.

Through the years, I saw dragonflies drying alongside their discarded coverings. I never saw one emerge from its larval case, but I hoped that someday I would witness the metamorphosis.

One tranquil morning in late May, I headed west off the Scenic Highway to Buckman Lake. The spring sun made the day feel soft and warm, and I was not in a hurry. While unloading the kayak, I sensed something wonderful in the air. There was no wind; the water was as smooth as a mirror. The air was dry. I scanned the shoreline and straight away noticed small ink dots on the stems of cattails and rushes. At first I did not think too much about the dots, but later I took a closer look and discovered that it was my childhood friends, the little dragons, who were responsible. Thousands of dragonflies were preparing to take a life-changing action step. The creatures, dark with wetness, did not discriminate. They clung to fresh green stocks and old brown ones too. Soon their protective coverings would dry, becoming brittle and crisp. I knew what was about to happen. I was fascinated and eagerly settled in to watch the show.

Of course, I had forgotten that Mother Nature carries a different watch than I do. Things progressed more slowly than my tolerance for sitting still allowed, so I paddled a bit, slipping in and out of the foliage while constantly monitoring progress.

When it happened, it happened quickly. At one of my checkpoints I saw where the thin larval armor had split just behind the head. In a backbend maneuver that would win gold at any summer Olympics, the squished-up body of the dragonfly slowly and painstakingly elongated to squeeze through the small opening. Then it pushed itself into an arch until its head was at the base of the shell. The wings unfolded like an origami puzzle coming to life.

Spellbound, I stared—not fully comprehending what I had just seen. All around the lake individuals were in various stages of emergence. I paddled ahead eager to find another spot to again watch and stare—amazed at the perfection of it all. The abdomen would un-kink, straighten out, and become round and full—similar to a balloon when it is blown up. While the wet wings shimmered and dried, the exhausted dragonfly was content to rest in the sun and prepare for life above water.

Astonished and amazed, I slowly made my way around the lake. Even if those brand new dragonflies had not shared their once-in-a-lifetime performance with me that day, I could not have been disappointed

in Buckman Lake. Along the shoreline were four or five beaver lodges in various stages of disrepair. Some were supporting small willow saplings, grasses, or any number of assorted and sundry plants that had found sufficient soil to get firm footholds. Through the clear water I spotted a snapping turtle resting peacefully on the bottom. A busy muskrat wove in and out of the cattails. Overhead, a pileated woodpecker flew its dippity-do flight. Two wood ducks waddled through the trees. A great blue heron waded in the creek that flowed into neighboring Marble Lake. I knew how fortunate I had been to be in the right place at the right time, and I was reminded of a favorite Mae West line: "Too much of a good thing can be wonderful."

"Too much of a good thing can be wonderful."
– Mae West

Two years later, on the first day of June, when the wind was whipping up white caps and the mercury stretched past 80 degrees, I took a trip north and east beyond Buckman Lake to Erickson Lake. No one came with me that day. I was running on my own time and schedule, traveling at an atypically leisurely pace.

Erickson Lake was at the end of a rough road that required four-wheel drive. It had been a slow year for leaves to emerge, so it was easy for me to find lakes just by looking through the woods. I left the truck parked at a mud hole that was large enough to float the kayak. The air was scented by the fresh smells of spring. Drooping yellow bellwort, always coy, hung their pretty heads. Perky violets, proudly dressed in white, yellow, and purple, decorated the forest floor. I did not mind carrying the kayak in the last quarter mile. The lake sparkled in the sun, reassuring me that it was nearby. Before long, I reached the shore and was soon on the water.

I am most open to reflection when I am alone on the water in my kayak. There I become a willing captive. It is never too easy for me to be still, but the rhythmic activity of paddling naturally lulls me into a meditative state. The gentle routine movement becomes unconscious at times, inviting thoughts to visit through subtle channels. The chipmunk chatter in my head all but disappears. I even quit starting and making lists. The listening is not just with my ears; my way-down-deep-inside secret places pay close attention too. I am just being, not wondering about motives or explanations or outcomes. Finally, it is safe to just let go.

Frequently, I have no idea what it is that I have heard or felt, if anything, until a few days, weeks, months, or even years later when a thought, feeling, or idea—seemingly from nowhere—becomes crystal clear …

maybe even second nature. By then I have silently incorporated a new behavior or belief into my life. The natural world often has that gentle effect. Those magic moments can also come and go like the wind.

> "I am most open to reflection when I am alone on the water in my kayak. There I become a willing captive."

Comfortably bobbing on the waves and communing with God, my reverie was suddenly broken when my eye picked up movement on a tree branch. Looking more carefully, I caught the bold, bright yellow spot on the tip of a cedar waxwing's tail. As if that was not enough, something glistened. Squinting, I looked hard but did not trust my naked eye. The bird was busy, but doing exactly what remained a mystery. Pulling out the binoculars, I took in every detail. The waxwing had snatched a dragonfly out of the air and was proceeding to devour it. The sun flickered off the dragonfly's transparent wings as they stuck out of the waxwing's bill. Then the waxwing caught and ate another dragonfly. Watching it twice made me a believer.

Wow! I had always imagined that my old friends the dragonflies were somehow exempt from being eaten. Because they were helpers, I figured they must be immune from predators. I never considered that they were part of the food chain. Perhaps the food chain did not distinguish between food and feeders as distinctly as I did. I just thought dragonflies died from old age or being T-boned by oncoming vehicles.

While kayaking, it is common to find dead or nearly dead dragonflies floating on the water's surface. I usually try to rescue them with my paddle, making a few failed attempts before successfully depositing them on the kayak deck. Sometimes it is just too late. But if they do have any life left in them, they will rest a while before taking off. When a curious, or more likely tired, dragonfly lands on my arm and rides along, it is a pleasant surprise. A select few prefer a higher vantage point, perching on my shoulder, hair, or even an ear. I never mind. Dragonflies are phenomenal friends. And I still believe in magic.

Mary uses binoculars to study the far shore on Carpics Lake.

Bitten

The coppery taste of warm blood filled my mouth. My knees were weak and shaking. Dozens of pinpricks jabbed my bare calves, shoulders, neck, and upper arms. The sun was setting, and I was frantically looking for the truck. I knew what had gone wrong, but it was way too late to fix it.

Needing to lighten my load, I set the kayak down by a tall black spruce and stumbled through the brush until I stepped out onto a snowmobile trail. Disoriented and needing to make better time, I took off jogging. It turned out to be in the wrong direction.

A few years before that evening my husband Gary and I had seen an ad for a piece of lakeshore east of Marcell on Egg Lake. Not wanting to waste time, and figuring everyone else would be racing to buy that very same property, we promptly jumped in his pickup and headed north. We intended to scout the land and put some money down. We appreciated the area lakes and dreamed of living on one. Gary wanted a peaceful cabin with a fireplace and a view of water. I had visions of stately pines alongside a pristine lake.

When we arrived at the for sale sign, we wished we had brought our boots. Some of the land was swampy and low, and the existing trees were planted after a recent logging operation had passed through. Disappointed, we did not explore extensively. Instead, we drove home via the little café attached to the laundromat in Marcell. Needing to soothe our souls, we ordered chocolate milkshakes and quickly sucked them down.

Afterward, I often wondered what the land might look like from the water and if we should have pursued it further. One hot July evening I decided to find out, and I borrowed Gary's truck for the trip.

There was no public access or makeshift landing to be found on Egg Lake, so I continued on to Forest Lake. The map showed a possible water route between the two. I needed to paddle both lakes, so it seemed like a win-win situation. Monstrous mosquitoes met me at the grassy pull-in located many yards away from the edge of the water. As usual, I was in a hurry to get going. I did not have hands enough to smack the little winged devils and carry the kayak through the brush at the same time. Wearing just shorts, strapped sport sandals, and a sleeveless T-shirt, I had plenty of skin exposed for bloodletting.

The shoreline was thick with mature cedar trees.

Eager to get away from the biting horde, I quickly launched the boat and paddled toward the middle of the lake. Away from shore, the mosquitoes thinned out, but the angry welts growing on my arms and legs begged to be soothed by something cool. Dipping my hands into the reddish water, I was instantly put off by the unnatural warmth that greeted my fingers. Disappointed, I gave up on getting any longed-for relief.

"Wearing just shorts, strapped sport sandals, and a sleeveless T-shirt, I had plenty of skin exposed for bloodletting."

I turned my attention to the map and went about finding, and then exploring, the inlet from Carpics Lake on the east side. I followed that waterway for a short distance, noting that it was both deep and wide but not at all inviting. Since it was already late, I did not pursue it further.

What I really wanted to find was the outlet to Johnson Lake on the north end of Forest Lake. Many times I had driven over its culvert on County Road 45, so I knew the outlet existed. Challenged by dense cattails and abundant lily pads, I could neither see nor paddle to an opening. I was aware that a lone loon pair had been swimming in the middle of the lake the whole time I had been there. A tinge of sadness passed through me when I saw they had no chicks.

Hoping there really was a channel into Egg Lake, I went to the southwest corner of Forest Lake and began searching. Hidden behind a broken-down beaver lodge was a wide passageway. From there, it was an easy paddle into 12-acre Egg Lake. I scanned the shoreline hoping to recognize the land Gary and I had so briefly visited. Locating it was not an easy task, so I ended up just pretending to know where it was. A grassy hillside on the east side caught my eye. It appeared to have been logged in the last few years. I wondered if that was the spot I was seeking. The setting sun shone on the slope suggesting a performance stage.

As if on cue, I sighted a hungry doe nibbling on foliage. The gentle evening light accentuated her rich orange coat. She was beautiful. With her back to me, the deer had no idea she was being watched. I studied her through my binoculars. Several silent moments passed. Her ears twitched nonstop trying to keep the flies away. The doe moved her jaw in an exaggerated sideways fashion as she chewed each mouthful. The over-emphasized action of her jaw reminded me of cartoon characters that would never master chewing with their mouths closed. The scene made me smile. Even after our initial eye contact, the animal continued

to eat. It was not until her second head turn that she got nervous and started stomping and snorting. I whistled. She bolted into the brush, waving goodbye with her white flag tail. Hearing the doe stomp her hooves and continue to snort made me grin. She was alarmed, and I was amused. In a twisted way I felt empowered, which was a good thing considering what happened next.

I returned to Forest Lake and began looking for my take out spot. I saw nothing familiar. Back and forth, back and forth, and back and forth again I paddled. The closer I got to the shoreline, the louder the buzzing, biting brigade became. Not having a better plan, I pulled onto the rocky shore and swiftly got out of the boat. With the kayak on my shoulder I started walking over the damp ground and through the cedar trees. My free hand slapped at all bare skin, but was unable to keep up with the mosquitoes' relentless assault. As I bumped along, gear fell out of the cockpit and landed with a thud. Stopping, I put the kayak down to secure the paddle, life vest, and camera bag hoping they would stay put. Suddenly I knew I had no time for games. It was then that I began looking for a landmark. Finding a large spruce tree, I set the kayak down. Figuring I might need a guide later, I grabbed the camera bag and struggled through the brush. When I came out on the snow-mobile trail, I set the bag down to mark the spot that would lead me back to my boat. By then I knew how critical a simple sign could be.

Even though I had both hands free to kill mosquitoes, I put all of my energy into jogging. Ignoring the pests, I concentrated on finding the truck. I heard a four-wheeler in the distance and instantly knew I was headed in the wrong direction. Doing a quick turn-around, I picked up the pace and began running. Soon I came to the camera bag, but I kept on going. Twigs, sharp grass, and raspberry bushes cut my skin, but I ignored the sting and kept moving. At last I saw the road where I had driven in. Breathless and bleeding, I made my way back to the camera bag. I locked my eyes on the top of the spruce tree and went in to retrieve the boat. Knowing where I was going encouraged me to calm down a bit, and carrying the kayak out slowed the pace. I stole a glance at my throbbing calves. They were black with biters. It looked as if there were way too many insects to kill, so I let them be. I became obsessed with devising a plan to load the boat as efficiently as possible. Finally, my eyes found the truck. I just wanted to get inside the cab and escape my relentless attackers.

Something else I really wanted to do was spit. The dry metallic taste in my mouth had become unbearable. Eventually, I worked up enough saliva to spew it out. Expecting blood, I was relieved to see that it was just the usual clear spittle. That puzzled me. Later,

a nurse friend told me that when our body releases adrenaline we experience the tang of metal in our mouths. Apparently what I tasted was raw fear, not blood at all.

Of course the only way I knew to get rid of that vile flavor was to eat a chocolate ice cream cone as soon as possible. And after donating so much of my blood to the mosquitoes, I figured I could really use some sugar. The closest, and by then the only still-open, ice cream opportunity was back in Marcell. The Pine Cone was a walk-up window where orders were taken. My favorite part about visiting the Pine Cone, besides the ice cream, was seeing the *Blue Book* fish listings of what types of fish had been caught, their weights, names of the lucky fisherpersons, and from which lakes the lunkers had supposedly been taken. All of that information was neatly handwritten on the brown chalk-board that stood under a light by the order window.

I scanned the fishing data while waiting for my cool treat. As a kid I had seen a lot of fish and knew about the *Fisherman's Blue Book* listings. In the summer, Dad and I made frequent trips to Voight's Resort Store on Deer Lake for root beer floats. The walls of Voight's, an official weigh-in station for the *Blue Book*, were lined with photos of happy tourists and locals proudly holding up their catches for the camera. That innocent memory made me smile and helped me feel more at ease. My confidence was returning.

From this vantage point, Mary visited all 1,007 lakes in Itasca County.

Common sense suddenly kicked in and told me to fill the truck with gas. The evening was not yet over, and I was not yet home. Instead of turning south I drove north on Highway 38 away from Marcell. At County Road 45 I turned east, headed for the culvert at the north end of Forest Lake. Some say that when you fall off your bike, the best thing to do is to get right back on it and pedal. That way you are not afraid of riding a bike again. I felt compelled to look Forest Lake in the eye and to cross the culvert. I needed a victory lap, and I wanted closure on the evening. I wanted to shift gears from a fearful feeling to one of knowing I had just learned a hard lesson. I knew full well that I would continue to explore. Forest Lake had been a wake-up call to pay better attention to what I was doing and to think a few steps ahead. In the future I would carry marker ribbon with me, and I would use it.

Cruising down the road, I savored the ice cream as it worked its soothing magic on my stressed soul. In the waning light I thought I saw something standing crosswise in the middle of the road. At first I could not figure out what it was because I had never seen such a creature in the woods before. The leggy little animal was tan, had a head like a Jersey calf, and a hump across its shoulders. With a loping gait it moved off the road and into the woods. I kept staring and eventually convinced myself I had been

watching a moose calf. I could hardly believe my eyes! I had never seen a moose in the wild, let alone a baby one. Once the awkward calf got into the trees a few feet, it stopped and began pulling at the leafy end of a low branch. I looked around hoping to see the mama moose, but did not. In the lingering twilight I drove over the culvert. The lake appeared peaceful and non-threatening. I began making my way back home.

Soon it was pitch black. Headlights were coming at me. I struggled to see and thought something had gone wrong with my eyes. Then I realized I needed to pull over and use the damp boat sponge to wipe blood and squished mosquitoes off the inside of the windshield so I could see where I was going. My bites itched, my skin burned, and I craved a shower. I reminded myself that the discomfort was temporary and a small price to pay compared to spending a night alone in the woods without proper gear.

Gary was asleep when I got home and left before I was up the next morning. I awoke to the sound of the phone ringing. It was Gary. He went on and on about encountering bloody mosquitoes in his truck. He reported needing to clean his hands when he got to the shop, and he wanted to know just what had happened the night before.

etter Than Breadcrumbs

Taking a lesson from Hansel and
Gretel, I wanted a foolproof system
for getting out of the woods. I dili-
gently tied pink ribbons on branches.
Pink was not picked because it is a
girl color; it was a color others were
not using. Hunters choose orange,
the paper company uses blue, and
green is too hard to see. Even when
there are other pink markers in the
woods, my trail is easy to identify.
My ribbons are about four feet off
the ground, within sight of one
another, and are tied so they can be
removed with one hand as I leave.

Periscope up! An otter pops out of the water on Pothole Lake.

Sea Monsters

As a teenager I read a short account about a large northern pike that lived in a Wisconsin lake. The newspaper article reported that the fish had stationed itself near a swimming raft and eventually bit a swimmer. My brain immediately interpreted the story as evidence of the existence of enormous flesh-eating, fresh-water sea monsters. From then on, sea monsters were anything real or imaginary that might be lurking just below the water's surface ready to bite off my legs, feet, arms, fingers, or head.

Reading *Jaws* did nothing to alleviate my fear. Although I understood that sharks lived in oceans, not Minnesota lakes, I became even more neurotic. Then my friends and I watched the scary movie based on the book. For months afterward, I checked the toilet bowl (and tank) for life-threatening creatures before pulling my pants down and backing my bottom over the seat. I did not swim in lakes for the remainder of that summer. And while I eventually got over the terror of toilet monsters, the mean memories of fish-fed anxieties have multiplied over the years.

Fear of sea monsters could be a very big problem for a woman who often kayaks solo. It is dread of encountering monsters, not drowning, that keeps me from swimming alone; and I am not likely to snowshoe or ski by myself on the ice in winter because evil serpents, if they are hungry enough, may work up the power to burst through. In spite of my worries, I have never actually witnessed a life-threatening sea monster attack, but I have had a few chilling encounters with creatures that inhabit Itasca County lakes and bogs.

One April afternoon, two years into my quest, I paddled 12-acre Alder Pond. The sparsely forested northern side of this shallow lake caught my eye. A beaver lodge extended from the bank into the water. Behind the stick-and-mud dwelling many saplings and small trees had been cut. As I studied the scene, I heard a loud whap! directly behind the kayak. I flinched and felt myself come off the cushion on which I had been sitting. Pulling my body into a protective crouch, I looked over the side of the kayak expecting to see the open jaw of the infamous northern pike from Wisconsin. I saw nothing. I looked for a swirl or rings of waves left behind by such a fish leaping out of the water, but again I saw nothing. When I spotted the swimming beaver, I laughed. I had been fooled. It had been my belief that beaver came out to cut trees and patrol their territory only at dusk, but I was mistaken. From then on, whenever I saw a beaver house or fresh cuttings, I told myself to be prepared for the slap of a defensive beaver on the prowl.

On another outing, I was startled to see an undulating line break the water's surface—a swimming garter snake I presumed. The sun, a blazing ball of orange, was near the horizon, and the lake was quieting down for the evening. It was time to get off the water for the day, but curiosity got the best of me. Instead of heading back to the access, I paddled toward the swimming mystery.

Once I was side-by-side with my snake, it transformed into a platter-size snapping turtle. The carapace of the large snapper stuck out a fraction of an inch above the water. Sawtoothed projections on the tail, which trailed behind the reptile and looked like a tiny rudder, also rode at the water's surface. The wiggling line of shell and tail moving back and forth on the water had tricked me. Within seconds of our meeting, the prehistoric creature dove and disappeared into the depths of Sand Lake. I cannot speak for the turtle, but I know I was relieved at that moment.

Seeing snakes has been a fairly common experience. On the average I have encountered two or three each paddling season. As I stepped out of the red pony (my red Chevy pickup) to open a gate one June morning, I noticed a garter snake coiled tightly near the gatepost. After I drove through and got out to

Loaded and ready to go, the red pony waits near Long Lake.

close the barrier behind me, I looked again and observed that the snake was no longer there. I wondered where it had gone so quickly, and I glanced around to be sure it had not slithered into the red pony.

> "I wondered where it had gone so quickly, and I glanced around to be sure it had not slithered into the red pony."

Sure that I had no uninvited company, I drove in the direction of Gorman and Fox Farm Lakes. When the road ended, I parked the truck, stuffed my pockets full of pink ribbons, and put on my fireman boots. I knew I would need the boots to cross the large wetland that stretched between dry land and the lake.

Immediately, the water was above my ankles. As I made my way through scrubby swamp willows and tag alders, I intentionally tied more ribbons than usual. Everything looked the same. As I considered where to step next, I noticed motion a few feet ahead. I gulped! The garter snake had reappeared, or one of its relatives had, and it was swimming at an angle across my intended path. I took a deep breath, told myself it was just a small reptile, and proceeded to wade through water that had reached shin depth. I

tied another ribbon and wondered how much farther I would get before the dark swamp water ran over the tops of my boots. I did not have to think about that too long. Already fidgety and hypervigilant from seeing one sea serpent, I let out a small scream when another snake headed in my direction. Leaving my tied ribbons behind, I splashed my way to shallower water and caught my breath. That was the moment I decided to buy hip boots.

Sea monsters do not have to be noisy, large, or slithery to be creepy. One warm spring afternoon Gary and I kayaked on part of the Hanson Lake chain. Wanting to investigate a creek bed as a possible portage route into Big Inky, the next lake south, we dragged the kayaks into a shady spot on the bank and began our pursuit on foot. The flowing water was shallow and mucky at first, but as we progressed we discovered a fairly clear little stream with steep black soil banks that reached above our heads. Gary did not mind wading in the creek bed, but I was more of a rock-to-rock jumper and fallen-log-balance-beam traveler that day. We finally reached Big Inky, but realized that we would have to find a different access some other time. Retracing our steps through and along the creek, we returned to our kayaks and paddled back to the landing spot.

Several hours later—after stopping for food and putting our gear away at home—we were ready to clean up. For some reason—possibly the intuition of a believer in sea monsters—I checked the shower after Gary stepped out. A shadow caught my eye. Crawling up the side of the shower wall was a short, plump, dark-brown leech. Then we noticed the trail of blood that Gary's foot was leaving on the bathroom floor.

Another memorable encounter with leeches happened on a Labor Day weekend when friends and I spent the better part of the day with an accommodating extended family and its trio of enthusiastic dogs. Half a dozen of us piled on our helpful hosts' four-wheel drive ATV, and several family members, along with the dogs, followed on the short jaunt to Herron Lake.

Horsethief Harry and I launched our kayaks in a narrow slice of murky brown water just wide and deep enough to keep us afloat. Once we had paddled out of the way, the dogs started playing in the stirred-up mix of water and mud. Our jovial friends stood talking in knee-high marsh grass while Harry and I made a quick tour around the clear, shallow lake. When we returned to the put-in spot, I noticed bright streaks of blood dribbling down the legs of the small white dog. I alerted the dog's owners, and a shrill shriek of "leeches!" was sounded. That brought the group to life. Some of the people were horrified, others were amused, but without exception, every individual there gave his or her own legs and feet a thorough inspection. Some of us checked more than once. By the time we had returned to our vehicles and loaded everything up, a total of 43 leeches had been pulled off the little white dog.

Needless to say, after 15 seasons of slogging across bogs, finding my way through forests, and kayaking on over 1,000 lakes, no sea monster has attempted to remove my legs, feet, arms, fingers, or head. But to this day I remain on alert in case I encounter such a creature. I figure it is just a matter of time.

Mature red pines catch the last of the day's sun at Scenic State Park.

Joy Lake

My birthday, for as long as I could remember, had always meant fun in the late summer sun; but it was raining the day I turned 40—a cool, slow drizzle that felt as if it might hang on for a long time. The weather and my mood were a perfect match: misty, gray, and damp; and the horizon showed no signs of getting brighter on either account.

Sixty-five miles from town, in the northeast corner of Itasca County, Joy Lake is secretly tucked away in a natural bowl. The 24-acre lake is surrounded by tax forfeited and paper company land.

Joy was not only welcome at that point in my life, it was also very desperately needed. Although the divorce was over on paper, it was not over in my heart. Aching for the old days of fun, frolic, and lighthearted exploration took up a considerable amount of my energy. I was in the beginning days of my solo journey and did not know—

or even pretend to believe—that I had the power to create and live out my own dreams. Friends and family members told me that 40 was when life began, but I did not believe that 40 held any magic. It did not seem to open a door to anywhere I wanted to go. Forty was more than I wanted to deal with any time soon.

As I turned onto a sandy two-track trail just off Rollercoaster Forest Road, my progress came to a halt. A dead balsam stretched diagonally across the path and blocked vehicle travel toward the lake. Apparently no one with a saw had used the road for a while, so I parked the truck and prepared to go the rest of the way to the lake, about 300 yards, on foot.

"Friends and family members told me that 40 was when life began, but I did not believe that 40 held any magic. It did not seem to open a door to anywhere I wanted to go. Forty was more than I wanted to deal with any time soon."

After unloading the kayak, I proceeded down the steep, sandy bank. My feet stopped where the hard ground ended. Joy Lake, surrounded by a tamarack and black spruce bog, had no cabins on its wet shoreline. A steep slope of mature red pines and white birch trees, set back from the water, rose up on the west side. Pine trees had always felt warm and safe to me. Ever since I was a young girl I had admired their strength and steadfastness. They were old friends that I was always glad to see. Just knowing that those stately pines would be watching over me was comforting.

It looked like a good 100 yards across the bog to the water. I could see that dragging the boat through the wet, grassy openness would be work. Tests of strength, endurance, and problem solving with the kayak would soon extend into other aspects of my new life. At that moment, however, I had no clue that one of my goals was to be a strong, independent woman. I was so overwhelmed by just surviving and trying not to cry so many times each day that clear thoughts about the future were scarce.

The overcast sky was thick, inviting darkness sooner than usual that evening. The haunting tremolo of a loon bounced off the pine-covered hill and reverberated back to me, breaking the silence. Unconsciously I wondered where that black and white diver was. Mist rose from the lake. I shivered, partly from the cool, moist air, but more from the mystic beauty that surrounded me. Out of respect for their fragility, I carefully stepped over pitcher plants. I passed by the puffy white heads of cotton grass and ended up goose-stepping my way through the knee-high blades of tapered sedge grass.

Slogging along in my not-so-dainty red and black fireman's boots and dragging the kayak loaded with my camera, water bottle, life jacket, and a spare sweater took maximum effort. Needing to catch my breath, I paused a moment.

Standing halfway between the high ground and the open water, I felt vulnerable and exposed. Both were familiar feelings those days. In fact, I often felt the same way in my own living room. I did not fear dropping a leg through the bog, but I always kept one hand on the kayak and the other tightly gripped around the paddle to stop myself from completely sinking out of sight if I fell through a hole. The distasteful thought of falling through a bog and becoming a snack for Swamp Thing was foremost in my mind when I made wetland crossings.

To compound my sense of alarm, I had a sudden irrational thought that a bull moose might appear. There were no trees to climb and no places to hide out there. In an effort to ease my panic and reconnect with reality, I spoke aloud. I told myself that I had not seen any moose tracks nor any moose-sized

droppings on the thick, reddish sphagnum moss. Self-talk helped ease my moose anxiety, so I tried to increase my confidence by reminding myself that most of my fears were unfounded. It worked. My anxiety drifted away, and I continued toward the lake.

Once again a loon yodeled. Just out of the mist, swimming side by side, a pair of mature loons caught my eye. Before long, they were straight out from where I was standing on the edge of the bog. "Even the loons have one another," I thought. Unlike me, they were not alone.

"Will I ever find a partner again?" I mumbled to myself for the umpteenth time that week.

I watched and listened as one loon began its familiar mournful call, and then the second joined in. I felt the echo pass through me, and another shiver bolted up my back.

When I finally reached the water I felt better. I knew my role in the kayak. I knew what to do and how to do it. How I would ever get the rest of my life to follow suit remained a question that went around and around in my head.

Before I forgot, I wanted to take the water clarity reading. "Where is my Secchi disk?" I wondered, feeling around with my foot on the bottom of the kayak.

I had forgotten to grab it out of the garage. I could not remember the simplest things. Where was my

The underside of a white water lily is perfectly reflected on the still surface of Little Island Lake.

brain? Was it still in my head, or had my aching heart also consumed the area between my ears?

Before long I was engrossed in grasping the reassuring hardness of the paddle as I glided along the bog rosemary and leatherleaf bushes. Smelling the faint fragrance of white water lilies and watching the silly antics of whirligig water beetles lured me back into the non-judgmental world of childhood. I longed for the old days at the resort on Bass Lake where I grew up.

When I was a child, one of my delightful adventures was rowing a 14-foot boat, all by myself, over to the lily pads. There I would bend over the transom and pull with all of my six-year-old might to secure a water lily for Mom. The round, slimy, green stem never broke off by the flower end. I usually ended up with a length of stem that rivaled my height. Just when I thought the stem had won our tug-of-war game, it would let go with a pop! and I would be on my backside across a boat seat—stunned, but still holding the trophy in my small fist.

I was so proud to have collected that treasure for Mom. Finding a low dish that held water, we would cut off the long stem and set the lovely lily inside. Our ritual was for Mom to tell me how beautiful the lily was. Then, she would give me a hug and a kiss to show her appreciation for my hard work and bravery. Deep in the lily's sweet-smelling yellow center were itty-bitty, crawly black bugs. Soon they made their

way up and out, crossing the petals to reach the edge of the flat dish and fall onto Mom's counter. That was pretty much the end for them, and not so long after, the end of the lily too. Like many things, it was fun while it lasted.

The sun found a single hole in the gray clouds and sent a beam of soft evening light onto a patch of tamaracks. Without conscious thought, I headed toward that sunbeam. I sensed the light would make this twilight paddle all the more healing. Mist still covered nearly half of the lake, the half into which I was headed.

"Just when I thought the stem had won our tug-of-war game, it would let go with a pop! and I would be on my backside across a boat seat—stunned, but still holding the trophy in my small fist."

My eyes followed a movement in the mist. The mature loons were not just a pair; they were also parents. Two adolescent chicks appeared, rounding out the loon family. The adult loons were attentive parents, and had very well-behaved teenagers, but as I watched them I was thankful I did not have offspring of my own for whom I needed to be responsible.

On the eastern edge of the lake, gumball-sized ruby red balls hung just above the water. Scantily fruited lowbush cranberry plants displayed the season's efforts. The berries hung like miniature Christmas ornaments and reminded me of all the thinly branched balsam saplings Dad and I had cut each year at Christmas time—always from a neighbor's woods, but never from our own. Mom always raised her eyebrows, but said not a word, as we happily dragged our skinny prize into the cabin to decorate it.

We were so pleased with ourselves. Perhaps the heavy air had muted all but the loons' trill on Joy Lake. Big picture thoughts came easily.

My breathing was slow and deep. As the kayak coasted along, I felt a smile spread across my face. Joy Lake had given me the opportunity to witness a peaceful loon family for an evening and to slow down long enough to get a sneak peek into the natural wonders of the bog. Recalling amusing memories of childhood had also helped. There had been no better birthday gift that year.

If I never paddled again, I knew that Joy Lake would have been the perfect spot to stop. It was no mistake that I had ended up there on my fortieth birthday—a birthday I had not been looking forward to at all.

As I left the lake, I raised my head and looked up. There, arched above the trail leading to the truck, hung a faint rainbow. I took it as a sign of good things to come. The rainbow was soft and beautiful. Silently, I began to shed tears. I had hope once again.

Mama Says

The aspen growth was so thick that I tied 42 pink ribbons to mark my way into an unnamed lake. On the trek out I decided to stray from my ribbon trail because I thought I knew a shortcut. It worked. I found the road, but when I got there I had no idea which way to go. Looking around, I spotted a mother porcupine with a tiny baby waddling behind her. I spoke to the pair, asking for help. The mother turned toward me. Her gaze seemed to say that I needed to go to the left. She was correct. Within 150 feet I found the truck exactly where I had parked it.

Pitcher plants' leaves collect water and insects.

Thirty Yards, My Ass

A colorful brochure for a rental cabin on Pine Lake caught my eye when I stopped at a local visitors' center. Pine was a lake I needed to paddle, but it did not have a public access. So I picked up a brochure and called the number listed.

What followed were several days of trading answering machine messages: a warm, chatty voice on one end and me on the other. On my first call I had introduced myself and asked permission to access Pine Lake. In one of the return messages, the friendly voice said that the property owners would like to paddle with me.

The idea seemed strange. Most people were agreeable when I approached them about getting to a lake through their property, but these were the first who said they wanted to go along. Did they want to spy on me?

As it turned out, John and Martha Hubbel joined me on Pine Lake and on more than 60 additional paddles. The first time I met them, I knew we were going to be friends. And it did not hurt that Maddie, their perky black Shih Tzu, and I bonded immediately. The Hubbels had been paddling a canoe together for more than 40 years. They were not nosy, just interested in making a new friendship with someone whose interests were similar to their own.

While we circled Pine Lake, we swapped camping, travel, and adventure stories. John had been an insurance salesman and Martha a preschool teacher. Conversation came easily—sometimes all three of us were talking at once. The beginning of a sweet friendship was sealed when Martha sent two jars of homemade jam home with me that day.

> "The beginning of a sweet friendship was sealed when Martha sent two jars of homemade jam home with me that day."

Topping the list of our most memorable outings was our trip to Lake Mary, John's idea for a perfect place to mark the halfway point in my 1,007-lake quest. It took a week's worth of phone calls and all of my hometown girl pull to make arrangements to access

the lake which was blocked off to the outer world by an orange gate with a thick padlock. Fortunately, the man who held one of the keys to the lock worked with the husband of my best friend from grade school. The Hubbels brought along houseguests, so our party consisted of five adults and two dogs. We traveled in three kayaks and one canoe.

Scenic Lake Mary, surrounded by an abundance of mature pines and only a few cabins, was home to a purplish-pink swimming raft. Although it seemed showy and gaudy in that northwoods setting, the raft turned out to be handy. A natural hostess and merrymaker, Martha suggested we stop at the colorful raft to have a treat.

"Why don't you climb up on that raft and get the ants out of your pants, Mary?" gracious and motherly Martha suggested with a twinkle in her eye.

Martha makes the best peanut butter and jelly sandwiches I have eaten in my adult life. She also bakes delicious gingersnaps and oatmeal raisin cookies. Anything from Martha's goodie bag is popular with the crowd, and it was time for a snack. So I paddled over to the raft, climbed aboard, and dragged my kayak up there with me so it would not drift away.

Much to my surprise, the Hubbels produced a bottle of sparkling champagne, plastic glasses, dried fruit, and nuts from their canoe. This was an official celebration in honor of paddling lake 500, they said.

A colorful pitcher plant flower brightens the Finn Lake bog.

As always, Martha had thought of everything. We toasted, drank up, and laughed; and John shared a colorful joke or two.

From the raft we paddled to the northwest shore of the lake. As we glided past a pair of loons we had the impression they were discussing whose turn it was to sit on their nest. Overhead, a pileated woodpecker caught our attention—alternately climbing and swooping—as it flew across the water.

We were drawn ashore at a cedar grove, a place where we determined the local pixies might dance and play. Protected by the cedars' heavy branches, the sloped ground was cool and shady, soft and mossy. A slightly sweet smell welcomed us, and our playful mood gained energy. Although we looked for the pixies and asked them to come out and do a jig, none appeared. That was when we all grew pretend wings, found our happy feet, and enacted our own elf-like capers. We danced and sang, and then we women ran and jumped—hoping to become airborne.

After paddling Lake Mary, we returned to our vehicles and prepared to leave. I invited everyone in the group to join me on Stumple and Whiskey, two small lakes that also lie behind the locked gate. Figuring this would be my only chance to reach those lakes, I felt I had to paddle them while I had the opportunity. The Hubbels' friends said they had enjoyed the trip so far, but had paddled enough for one day. John

and Martha decided to go to the lakes with me, and Maddie did not get to vote. Sending the heavy canoe home with the visitors, we loaded up the kayaks, gear, and dogs.

Following the two-track road away from Lake Mary, we peeked through the woods and spotted tiny Stumple Lake at the bottom of a hill. The incline had been logged recently, leaving behind many stumps, downed trees, and brush piles. John and I half carried and half dragged our kayaks down the hill while Maddie, on her rope leash, was hell-bent on pulling Martha toward the lake as quickly as possible. A small dog does not take into account that the human at the other end of the leash cannot squeeze under fallen logs, or that two legs cannot go as fast as four. Pulled along at a half trot, Martha worked frantically to untangle the leash when Maddie made passes around tree stumps or through brush. It was not easy going.

Between the logged area and the water, Stumple Lake was surrounded by a lowbush cranberry bog, a few stunted tamarack trees, and cotton grass. Our route was wet, and so were our feet. Quite a few scratches and "Oh, shits!" after entering the bog, we made it to the water's edge. Looking back to encourage his wife, who clearly had all she could do to keep up with Maddie, John shouted, "Just another 30 yards to the lake, Martha!"

Shortly after John and I put the kayaks in the water

and started paddling, we heard a reply. Angelic, generous, and thoughtful former nursery school teacher Martha yelled back, "Thirty yards, my ass! A hundred and thirty yards is more like it!"

It is hard to argue with the truth or with Martha Hubbel. John and I took our time on the water hoping that she would calm down, and she did. Later, we paddled Whiskey, a clear lake with many minnow traps, a pair of resident loons, and a shoreline decorated with clusters of pitcher plants and festive pink bog laurel flowers that reminded me of pinwheels at a Mexican fiesta.

My friends the Hubbels helped make the midpoint of my kayaking adventure an unforgettable day, and from that time on "Thirty yards, my ass!" was our code phrase for lakes that were difficult to reach.

An alert painted turtle casts a perfect reflection.

The Farm

One late afternoon in the summer between my kindergarten and first grade years, Dad announced that he was hungry for chicken and would be taking Mom and me to The Farm for dinner. We climbed into the car and drove for what seemed like forever past tall green pines, brown cattail marshes, and rolling hay fields. Then we drove a little bit more. By the time we pulled into a sloping driveway, I was not only bored, but also starved. In an instant, those concerns were forgotten as I took in the fascinating surroundings. The yard, full of rusting old wrecked cars and vans, along with a bus, was unlike anything my five-year-old eyes had seen before.

The three of us got out of our car and headed into the low building. Odors of frying food and cigarette smoke hung in the air as we walked in and found a table in the restaurant section. Off to the side, in a dark area we could not see well, we heard bar noises. Everything in the oblong room was turquoise, including the bikini-style top and scanty shorts that made up our waitress' Robin Hood outfit. She was in costume from head to toe. Her footwear matched her narrow, pointed hat—the only difference was that the hat had a single slender feather attached at an angle. My head whirled as I wondered what kind of a fairyland my parents had brought me to. I was not at all alarmed. On the contrary, I was intrigued.

As we waited for our chicken to arrive, a funny-smelling man staggered toward our table, invited himself into the fourth chair, and sat down. He smiled, and the next thing I knew, he pulled a quarter out from under my collar. Then he found another one behind my ear, and a third coin appeared from beneath my elbow. Totally amazed, I stared with my mouth agape. I was spellbound, but Mom quickly moved into action. Instead of telling me to say "Thank you," she made me give all of the money back to the magic man. Although I do not recall much more about that evening, I have replayed the scene in my head many times.

Two decades later my brother mentioned something about a fire that destroyed a chicken ranch up in the whistle-stop of Spring Lake. Things must have gotten really hot up there.

More years passed. I was in my early forties and found myself at a modest home on the shore of Spring Lake. It was a wet, gray June evening, and I harbored hopes of finding someone who would grant me permission to access the lake through the yard. Chatter drifted through the open kitchen window, accented by the sounds of kids playing in the suds as they cleaned up the supper dishes. Before I could reach the porch, Rocky, the man of the household, headed out to meet me. Seeing the kayak on top of the truck, he not only knew what I wanted, but he also recognized me. A year earlier, I had bought ice cream from him at the Spring Lake Store and picked his brain regarding area lakes. Across the road from his driveway sits the store where gas, bait, and other essentials share creaking wooden floor space with the Spring Lake Post Office.

Rocky was very accommodating. He directed me to drive down closer to the water and said not to leave anything unattended because his hyper brown dog would carry it off. Indeed, when my red life jacket fell off the tailgate, the dog grabbed it before it hit the grass. In a red flash, it was gone. Rocky soon retrieved both the dog and the life jacket. While helping me launch the boat, he mentioned that I should look out for deadheads.

Deadheads are sunken or partially sunken logs. On Spring Lake they offer evidence that both beaver and lumberjacks had been there. Not only did the deadheads slow me down that evening, they made me pay close attention to all of my surroundings. It was a perfect setting for introspection.

Drifting along near the south shore of Spring Lake and staring into the tangled roots of upturned trees,

I became very aware of how twisted and complicated one's time on the planet can become. It occurred to me that I no longer considered Gary a part of my life. We had shared many happy times, and he had taught me a great deal about paddling and being quiet on the water—behavior that had become my habit in the kayak. But I had reached a point where I was managing well alone. I was actively seeking my own adventures and fulfilling my own dreams. Many areas of my life were flourishing. Just as I began to appreciate my feelings of independence, I realized that I was lonely. The sudden unwelcome thought made me wince. I set my paddle across the cockpit of the kayak, drew my knees to my chest, and rocked myself.

Tears flowed and many minutes passed as I slipped into the private labyrinth of my thoughts and emotions. Finally, while still floating among the deadheads, I gave myself gentle permission to consider dating.

"I was actively seeking my own adventures and fulfilling my own dreams."

It began to rain—not hard, yet enough to create rings on the water and spots on my glasses. I was not in a hurry. I was still absorbing the idea of daring to seek an intimate relationship when I paddled by a beaver lodge and wondered if beavers were residing there or not. Unanswered questions intrigue me. For someone who always wants to know why, the status of the beaver lodge gave me a reason to think about something other than myself. The difference between this musing and hundreds of others was all about the degree of intensity. I would soon forget the beaver lodge, but would always remember the moment I contemplated having a companion again.

The dog had taken shelter by the time I returned to shore and the waiting truck, but reliable Rocky reappeared. As he good-naturedly helped me load up my kayak and gear, I started asking him a few questions. "Had he ever heard of a place up in this neck of the woods that served chicken dinners many years ago?" I wondered.

Yes, he knew of it.

This was the first time anyone, in all my years of inquiring about the chicken ranch, had ever confirmed my memories. Immediately, and with great enthusiasm, I launched into the whorehouse story Dad used to tell, including the part about the whoring happening in all the old cars, vans, and buses parked in the yard of the establishment. Eventually I remembered my manners and fell silent after apologizing to Rocky for keeping him out in the rain.

He made a funny face and said, "I used to own that place."

My first thought was to thank God that I had already paddled the lake. I apologized for my bluntness, and Rocky told me more. In the mid-sixties, the same era in which I had visited The Farm, but well before Rocky owned the place, the owners had lived in the Twin Cities for a time. While they were absent, their managers had let things run loose. Rocky and I parted on friendly terms.

A couple of years later I was back in Spring Lake scouting for lakes, and I stopped at the store to buy a soda. A middle-aged man was behind the counter. In the course of our conversation, he mentioned that he knew the area fairly well. So I asked if he remembered a place called The Farm. He said he did. Without hesitation, he gave me directions to where the building had once been.

I went exploring and found a driveway that passed between two old posts with remnants of tangled barbwire fence still clinging to them. The short road gently sloped and came to an end near a shed with a fallen-in roof. There was a hint of the old business; the ground was littered with rust-covered trucks and weathered farm equipment. Respecting the no tres-passing signs, I did not linger—stopping only long enough to see through adult eyes the place I remem-bered from my childhood.

 oxy Baby

Picking yet another wood tick off my
sleeve and dropping it over the side
of the kayak into Little Dick Lake,
I look up to see a brilliant red fox
standing on the steep brushy bank.
It is April. There is no leaf cover and
the early evening sun gives the fox
an amber glow. We stare at one another for what seems like minutes. I
feel his presence and know this fox is
my recently deceased father gently
watching me. Dad befriended a wild
fox when I was a kid. He often talked
about his beautiful Foxy Baby. The
neighbors thought he was seeing
another woman on the sly, but Mom
was not worried. She and Foxy Baby
were friends too.

The ruffed grouse takes its name
from the dark ruffs on its neck.

Curly

Sometimes the only way to access a small lake that lies near a county line is to drive into the neighboring county and use the available roads. A few times on purpose, and many times by mistake, I wove my way in and out of Itasca County.

Beltrami County is one of Itasca's neighbors to the west. It was named after an Italian naturalist, author, and explorer, Giacomo Costantino Beltrami. In 1823 Beltrami traveled through the area that would later be called Minnesota. He claimed to have discovered the headwaters of the Mississippi River although it was actually Henry Schoolcraft who identified Lake Itasca as the river's source. From my own experiences in the woods, I understand how Mr. Beltrami might have miscalculated.

It was spring. My calendar was clear and I was in the mood for some driving, so I headed west from Grand Rapids for a good hour and a half. Traffic was light. Even though Big Brother Bob and I had tried to fix the truck's antenna four times, the radio was not working, so I spent most of the ride looking out the window and silently daydreaming. When I finally arrived in Beltrami County, I did not meet an Italian, but I danced with a dog.

First on my list that Saturday was Skimerhorn Lake, a lake with a peculiar name that made me smile. An old woodsman told me that a skimmerhorn (two m's) was a ladle-like tool used by lumberjacks to scoop scum off the tops of liquids, but I did not learn what kinds of liquids. *The Third River Story*, chronicled by Lyle G. Lauber and written primarily by descendants of the first settlers who lived in that area, said that a Mrs. Skimerhorn (one m) from Michigan lived on Skimerhorn Lake. The book credited her with naming nearby Moose Creek. Perhaps she named Skimerhorn Lake too.

On my first visit to Skimerhorn the previous November, the water had frozen over and the surrounding vegetation was winter brown. This day, the lake was wide open. Grass at the carry-in boat landing was green again, already past my knees, and alive with wood ticks. The ticks wasted no time locating me and crawled up my pant legs in droves. As I paddled along, I kept picking them off my clothes and dropping them in the chilly water. I wondered whether fish eat ticks.

Scanning the grassy shoreline with binoculars, I saw a brown mammal deliberately chewing

"When I finally arrived in Beltrami County, I did not meet an Italian, but I danced with a dog."

something yellow. Apparently wanting a little more fiber, its mouth went around the pointed end of a narrow finger of gray driftwood. Unable to bite off the tip, the plump animal gave up, sensed my presence, scampered through the weeds, and disappeared into the lake. My eyes followed the faint V on the water's surface made by the swimmer below. I was unsure if the animal was a beaver or an overweight otter. When an otter raised its head above the water, the mystery was solved.

After paddling Skimerhorn, I headed farther west. Because I had not had human contact since the day before, I wanted to talk to someone. Crossing into Beltrami County also made 98 percent of my maps useless, so I felt a need for assistance. I pulled into one of the first driveways I came to. The place seemed friendly and looked busy with tractors, logging trucks, and other assorted big equipment parked around the large yard. The first sign of life I saw was two men who were standing on scaffolding and installing siding on the house. I remembered how a college professor had once embarrassed me in front of the whole class by announcing, "Never assume, Mary, it makes an ass out of you and me." Not heeding his advice, I threw caution to the wind and assumed that the two fellows were the homeowner and his grown son. I got out of the truck and began asking questions about the road to Marie Lake. Before they could tell me they were hired help and did not live around there, they began laughing.

Without warning, a big, black, tail-wagging farm dog mounted me and was enthusiastically humping the entire left side of my body. The siding guys roared. Between bursts of laughter, they directed me to the side door to find the homeowner. The animal locked its paws on my shoulders. I did my best to avoid his slobbering tongue while we danced toward the house. We were about the same height.

Leaning through the doorway, a man shouted, "Curly, go lie down!"

Fortunately, the dog obeyed. Out of breath, I staggered into the farmhouse and tried to regain my dignity; but by then I was laughing too.

Never mentioning the actions of his dog, the man invited me into the kitchen. He pulled out his Beltrami County map, which we studied together, and then he gave detailed instructions about which local roads to travel and which to avoid. When his kind wife entered the room, she looked at me for a moment and then said, "You have a tick crawling up your pants. Oh no! It just went under your sweater."

In the process of pulling that tick off, I found another one. Reaching out her hand, she said, "I'll take those."

Handing her the two ticks, I remarked, "Well, if this isn't Minnesota hospitality, I don't know what is."

She smiled and took the ticks to an ashtray where she burned them.

Before I left the safety of the porch, I scanned the yard for Curly. Not seeing him, I hurried toward the truck. I was no more than a third of the way there when I heard the homeowner holler, "Watch your back! Here comes the dog!"

This time I had a plan. Turning sideways, I shoved my knee between Curly and my body. I let him have his way; I was saving my strength for the end. We hopped to the truck door where I gave the enthusiastic creature a hearty push that knocked him on his backside. That gave me enough time to jump into the cab and slam the door before he could stand up. The siding guys cheered. As I pulled out of the driveway I glanced in the rear view mirror. A forlorn Curly was watching me speed away.

The man had given me sound advice about walking into Marie Lake before attempting to drive down the deeply rutted and muddy two-track-trail that led to the water. I could not decide if I should risk getting stuck, or if I should just carry the boat in. I was distracted by the crescendo of a ruffed grouse drumming—a thump, thump, thump mating ritual created by the bird beating its wings rapidly. The sound always reminds me of a diesel engine trying to start again and again and again. The message I heard in the grouse's rhythm was that I should build a bridge, put the truck in four-wheel drive, go slowly, and everything would be fine.

The well-worn grooves in the road were almost knee deep. Others before me, probably fishermen or hunters, had laid short log sections in the ruts. I looked around the area for what else I could employ as filler. A few old tires were scattered in the woods, but I did not want to use them. Fortunately, I spotted two heavy planks of wood. It was nearly all I could do to drag the four-by-eight, eight-foot-long planks into the ruts to create a passageway of sorts. Out of the corner of my eye, I spotted a large cedar tree I could attach a tow strap to if I needed to use a winch to crank myself out of the mud hole.

The grouse's message turned out to be right. The truck had no trouble crossing my homemade bridge.

All of the effort to get into Marie Lake was worth it. Before I even got out from behind the steering wheel, I spotted a floating line of white on the far side of the 45-acre lake. Nervous and noisy, a pair of swans headed up a procession of swimmers that also included three calm, collected pelicans. Two immature bald eagles, each sitting in a different tree, took flight at the same time. A peeping squadron of yellow and brown fluff balls sneaked through the rushes under the watchful eye of Mother Mallard, and a green heron flew along the shore. The colorful and vocal assortment of swimming and flying birds was both entertaining and welcome company. It was a beautiful sight, punctuated by the distant continuous sound of the drumming ruffed grouse.

Curly was not the only one looking for a date that day.

omething Fishy

As we approach the cobweb-cluttered culvert leading into Lower Hanson Lake, Gary and I think we hear voices. It is hard to say because we also hear flowing water and calls from redwing blackbirds. We point to the opening, then become silent and resume paddling. The current is moderate, so negotiating the narrow, dark culvert is not difficult. Spilling out of the opening, we land in a minnow seine. The two men wearing waders are startled, to say the least, when they catch a pair of kayakers in their net.

A beaver lodge and colorful fall foliage create a peaceful picture, giving no clue that a tornado warning has been posted for the Stumple Lake area.

Spirit Waters

It was a spirit lake. The hair on my arms stood up. My stomach tightened. A shiver raced down my neck. I did not know why, but I did not like what I felt; and I was definitely on high alert. If John and Martha Hubbel had not been with me that sunny Labor Day afternoon, I would have sped to the middle, taken a Secchi disk water clarity reading, and then spent the next 60 seconds looking over my shoulder and paddling as quickly as I could to get out of there.

I swung the kayak around to watch the Hubbels paddle their green canoe through the makeshift culvert I had just come through and wondered how long it would take before they said anything about where we were. As usual, Maddie, their beloved Shih Tzu, was stretched out on her trapezoid-shaped riding platform. Maddie's perch was securely braced to the bow gunnels, just in front Martha's knees.

Squinting, I scanned the side of the lake in my immediate line of vision hoping to pick up clues to explain why I wanted to leave. The majority of the visible shoreline

Curious and friendly, this pair of Christmas Lake loons comes close to the kayak.

Eggs

Dad took me to a Rolls Royce dealership in Pasadena, California when I was a child. I clearly remember him saying, as we walked through the door, "Put your hands in your pockets; and, by God, do not touch a thing in here!"

For the most part, I apply my father's admonition as I traverse the lakes, bogs, and wooded areas in Itasca County. Mother Nature has shared many wonderful surprises with me over the years. I try to repay her kindness by leaving things as I find them, but sometimes it is hard to avoid the temptation to touch—especially in the spring.

Winter often overstays its welcome in northern Minnesota. When snow-packed trails and chilly temperatures finally depart, I long to be outside. A beautiful spring day is one of Mother Nature's finest gifts—plump with possibilities and an invitation to explore.

On a sunny morning in early May, as the temperature finally climbed above 50, the red pony and I traveled to the woodsy, wet ground between Wirt and Marcell.

Full of energy and enthusiasm that I had been saving since the lakes froze over the previous fall, I was eager to get started. When I reached a place where I could park the truck, I quickly unloaded the kayak and started my trek toward Rock Lake. Dainty white and yellow violets colored the brown forest floor—a floor many layers deep with decayed leaves from seasons gone by.

Without emerging foliage to clutter the view, it was easy to see through the woods and pick up a trail. Even though the lake was straight ahead of me, I could tell it would take some negotiating to get there. What once had been the shoreline was now a muddy slope. The area had received minimal precipitation over a period of years, and a dilapidated and leaking beaver dam had allowed some of the remaining water to escape. As the water retreated, the area around the lake became a quagmire. Duck tracks, mixed with those of shore birds and small mammals, punctuated the black muck. About 20 feet of soft, sticky terrain separated me from Rock Lake.

By dragging rotten sections of downed trees from the high ground and adding a few rocks and an armload of brush, I was able to construct a crude yet sturdy bridge that allowed me to carry the kayak across the mud and set it down in the tea-colored water.

As I pushed and paddled away from shore, dozens of long-abandoned beaver sticks, made bare by the receding water level, scraped along the kayak. At one time I might have cringed at the sound, but the kayak and I had traveled many miles together and I was used to finding scratches and rub marks on her surface.

A gaggle of Canada geese, making a terrible racket, congregated in the western pocket of the tiny lake. It sounded as if the geese were scolding. Most likely, I thought, the honkers did not want a visitor.

My normal pattern was to circle a lake along the water's edge, but in this case it was just too shallow. Instead, I headed toward a beaver lodge in the middle of the lake. This also moved me away from the distressed geese.

As the kayak glided toward the pile of sun-dried sticks and mud, a Canada goose raised her head and began squawking at full volume. Feathers flew as she frantically flapped her wings. Her blustery response to my arrival seemed foolish. Perfectly camouflaged while warming her eggs—with wings tucked in and head down—she might have gone undetected had she remained silent. Instead, she blasted off the nest like a Fourth of July firecracker.

It is not uncommon to see geese, and sometimes even loons, nesting on abandoned beaver lodges. I have considered that industrious beavers would be wise to hire business managers to collect rent checks and deposit them in a beaver bank.

After the disgruntled goose joined the rest of the flock, I landed the kayak on the lowest flat ledge of the lodge. My intent was to photograph the cluster of eggs and leave quickly, but as I neared the nest my plan changed. Shallow, bowl-shaped, and softly lined with white down, the dinner plate-sized nest held a treasure of five cream-colored eggs. I observed that mother goose had been more concerned with efficient incubation practices than housekeeping. Organic matter, perhaps from her underside, stained the eggshells.

"My intent was to photograph the cluster of eggs and leave quickly, but as I neared the nest my plan changed."

Although I felt it was wrong, I was tempted to reach down and touch one of the magic ovals. I gave in and dropped to my knees. The egg was warm and drew my chilled hand into the nest. Softly stroking its smooth surface with the backs of my fingers, I sensed the strong commitment of the goose as she tried to fulfill her primal duty to populate northern Minnesota with goslings. As soon as I removed my hand, I felt remorse about violating such a sacred space and for leaving my scent on the egg. I hoped the goose would return.

After my experience on Rock Lake, I did a little research. Ornithologists say that most birds have a limited sense of smell, so it is unlikely that the goose would have abandoned the nest merely because I touched an egg. Her mother instincts would have been too strong. In any case, my sense of guilt about touching the goose eggs was not enough to deter me when I encountered a different kind of nest years later.

On another mild spring day, a friend helped me tow and tug the kayak into an unnamed lake in the northwestern part of the county. We wheeled the craft down an old logging road and across a field before removing it from the cart and lugging it through a birch grove and up a steep hill. After that, we followed a creek bed to the point where there was more water than hard ground. From there I pushed alone through a bog that was too thick to allow the kayak to float, but wet enough that the water ran over the tops of my boots.

When I finally reached the lake, I was happy to climb into the kayak and start paddling. As I went around a point of bulrushes, I noticed movement to my left. I watched a loon steal off its nest and slip under the water, and then I paddled closer. From the kayak, I could see one egg. Loons' nests intrigue me, but I try

A loon hunkers down on its nest to avoid detection.

to maintain a respectful distance when I see them, in part because loon reproduction rates are low. Females lay only two eggs per season. I also enjoy the occasional company of loons when I am paddling. While ducks and geese tend to retreat when they see the kayak, loons will sometimes surface nearby. They seem to be interested in who, or what, is sharing their lake, and they are not shy about cruising over for a closer look—sometimes getting within 10 feet of my kayak. Occasionally they let out a soft, sweet hoot. I like to think that means we are friends.

As I continued the trip around the lake I heard a commotion in the distance and looked up to see a pair of trumpeter swans flying away from a brown clump in a grassy area. Curious about what they had been doing there, I decided to investigate. Nearing the area where they had been, I realized that the low mound of grass and floating vegetation was their nest. It was about four feet across and looked strong enough to hold me. I landed the kayak, scrambled out, and stared into the shallow depression. Six off-white eggs, each about four and a half inches long, lay clustered together. The urge to touch was overwhelming. I checked the sky. The swans were nowhere in sight, and Dad was not there to say no, so I gently brushed the warm eggs with my fingertips. Once again I felt guilty for invading a nest.

Maybe everyone feels a need to be naughty from time to time. After my father's warning, I did not pat a fender or smudge a bit of polished chrome in the Rolls Royce showroom. Yet many years later—when no one was around to see—I got away with something that was simultaneously wonderful and mischievous. My guess is that very few humans have had the chance to see, let alone touch, goose or swan eggs in the wild. I was fortunate to have been on the right remote lakes at opportune times. Touching twice was enough. I will leave it at that, always remembering the feeling of those warm eggs against my cool fingers.

Two newly hatched eastern kingbirds and one spotted egg share a nest on Simpson Lake.

ervous Kingbirds

A pair of nervous eastern kingbirds
fluttered about as I approached
a dead tree that hung into the water.
Usually kingbirds perch on the high-
est tree branch, so seeing their fran-
tic flight was a tip-off that something
was amiss. Soon I discovered the
reason for their anxiety. Just a few
inches above the water, cradled in a
V of two branches, was their cup-like
nest. Construction materials included
twigs, rootlets, and dry weed stems.
Peeking inside, I saw that two eggs
had hatched; the third was not visibly
cracked. I reached for my camera.
At the sound of the shutter, the two
babes pointed their gaping, hungry
mouths toward the lens. I quietly
paddled away and left the feeding
chores to the parents.

After paddling DNR Lake #940 on a cold afternoon in May, Mary drags her kayak back to the truck.

Flipped Out

I was lucky the day turned out as well as it did. Things could have been far worse. None of the mishaps would have occurred if I had simply slowed down.

Early that Friday morning I had taken my mother to the Duluth airport so she could fly home to Arizona after a month-long visit. The rest of the day was open and all mine. I was ready for adventure and eager to paddle, so I headed to unknown territory in the swampy north central region of the county.

The first four or five hundred lakes were fairly easy to find and get to. After eight years of paddling, however, I was on my way to lake number 632. No one knew where I was going or when I might return—this trip took place before I started leaving my day's itinerary and a map on my kitchen counter when I left home. As it turned out, it was the last trip I did as a free agent.

Although it was mid August, the temperature barely reached the low sixties. The wind felt determined and powerful. Loose leaves blew across the road ahead of me, and small branches danced wild jigs in the treetops as gusts rushed through.

After leaving the Scenic Highway, I traveled along County Road 344 for a good half dozen miles before I found the logging road I anticipated would be there. My attention was divided between the road and the plat book and maps at my side. It was not long before I came to a barrier.

"No one knew where I was going or when I might return— this trip took place before I started leaving my day's itinerary and a map on my kitchen counter when I left home. As it turned out, it was the last trip I did as a free agent."

The first downed tree was a six-inch balsam that did not yield to the dull edge of my single-bladed axe. I almost gave up at that point. Swinging hard did nothing more then bounce the axe head away from the tree trunk and sideways onto my shin. Ouch! I was glad I was wearing long pants. A few choice words escaped my lips as I wiped stinging tears from my eyes. I limped around to the bed of the truck and pulled out the Swede saw. After cutting my hand on the blade, I slowed down and finished the tree-removal job wearing gloves. The cautionary advice of a wise old Finn applies to every situation: "Use your head and your body won't suffer!"

At each Y in the road I followed what looked to be the more traveled route, although some routes looked as if they had not been traveled in a long time. The good news was that the mud puddles were not deep enough to require four-wheel drive. After the third stop to cut trees out of the road, I kept the saw up front with me so I would not have to waste time returning it to the back of the truck only to retrieve it again. Finally, I spotted a no trespassing sign that meant I was headed to someone's deer shack or the lake was close. The road narrowed. After clearing away one more tree, I drove up to a single cabin. There was a swing set in the yard and a new wooden dock.

It was nearly noon. I wanted to act quickly so I would not be caught trespassing by the cabin owners should they arrive for the weekend. Feeling victorious about finding Steel Lake and fueled by adrenaline from playing lumberjill on the drive in, I hastily unloaded the kayak and gear and carried it all down to the dock. Oblivious to danger, I launched into wild, wind-driven whitecaps.

On a rainy May morning, Mary paddles up the creek into DNR Lake #941.

Even though the sun was out, the air was chilly. It felt good to be wearing a thick wool sweater as I paddled along near the edge of the weeds. Within the first hundred yards of leaving the dock, I noticed something on shore to my right. Wanting to have a closer look I canted the kayak downwind to the left. Leaning the opposite direction one wants to turn a kayak lifts the tip and tail of the boat out of the water to afford a quicker turn. The turn was immediate, just not how I intended it to be. I was turning over, not to the right.

As I fell out of the kayak and into the water, my first thought was, "How the hell can this be happening to me, the famous Kayak Lady?" My next thought was, "The sea monsters will eat me!"

The kayak was about to completely flip and come down on top of me. With a tremendous surge of upper body strength, I gripped the cockpit rim and pushed the craft upright; then, in one fluid, urgent movement swung my legs and torso back inside. It all happened in less than the blink of an eye. I was amazed and alarmed, but not panicked; and I was sitting in four inches of clear, chilly water.

Doing a quick inventory, I realized that my binoculars in their gray protective case were gone. At once I became angry with myself for being so reckless—not so much for tipping over, but because I had lost the binoculars. They were good quality and fit my hands

and eyes perfectly. In that ice-cold moment, their importance became crystal clear. The binoculars had been the last tangible gift from my former husband. I cherished those little field glasses.

In my mind's eye I remembered distinctly. Gary and I had been getting along well the day he gave me the binoculars for my birthday. I knew he had made an effort to find me a gift I really needed and wanted. The nowhere-to-be-found gray bundle said, "Yes, he did love me. Yes, he did care."

As fast as a whitecap could flip a kayak, the final strand of connection to Gary had disappeared and drowned.

Just when I felt miserable inside and out, the binoculars and my camera floated down from the bow and bumped into my knee. I was so relieved. All I could do was pluck them up, watch them drip, and thank my God that they were still in the boat and not in the lake.

I shivered as the reality of my situation sunk in. I had to get to shore quickly, but it was going to be difficult without a paddle. My teeth chattered as I looked over my shoulder and caught sight of the blade floating a kayak length away in approximately the same spot where the kayak had almost turned over.

Deciding it was better to retrieve the paddle than to keep holding the drenched camera and binoculars, I dropped the pair back in the watery cockpit. Using my hands to propel the kayak, I went after the paddle and soon was able to grab it. By then I was freezing, and my waterlogged wool sweater had grown heavy. Paying full attention to what I was doing, I carefully angled the kayak into the whitecaps and returned to the dock.

Once safely on dry ground, I pulled everything out of the boat, including the wet lifejacket stuffed behind the seat. Between the fresh breeze and fear, I had begun rocking with violent shivers. I stripped to the skin and was blown dry before I could find a towel. My truck became a makeshift clothesline, its flat warm hood a perfect drying rack for the soaked camera and those beloved binoculars. People always teased me about having almost anything stowed behind the truck seat. Fortunately for me that day, I found a complete set of dry clothes including rubber moccasins and another wool sweater that I promptly pulled on.

Shielded by the truck and out of the wind, I refueled with a bottle of water and ate an orange. Seeking warmth and protection, I hunkered down in the sun and stared at the angry lake for a few minutes. My choices were to pack up and go home, or to bail the kayak, get right back into it, and paddle around the lake. I chose the latter while I still had the courage to do so.

I do not recall much about Steel Lake itself, and I did not discover what had initially caught my eye. After mentally replaying the scene over and over again, I realized that many factors had joined forces to roll the kayak. Trying to turn in whitecaps in a hurried fashion was the critical contributing error. Using a new, unfamiliar paddle that caught the water more sharply than I was accustomed to and not respecting the gusty wind did not help either. My not-to-be-forgotten lesson from Steel Lake was that even the always-in-a-rush Kayak Lady—the woman with the large head and ego to match—was not immune to calamity. After my wet adventure on Steel Lake, I became much more cautious on the water.

The camera never worked well again; but after a trip to the factory and a $17 repair, the binoculars were as good as new and have remained by my side.

I learned some valuable lessons on the trip to Steel Lake. Of course it would have been easier if I had followed the old Finn's advice in the first place: "Use your head and your body won't suffer."

October snow collects on a large beaver lodge.

ishhook Lake

Snow falls softly, muting all sounds. The October air is cool. Paddling through the snowflakes, I note the smooth, peaceful surface of the dark water. Fishhook Lake's boggy west edge is a maze of smoky gold tamaracks and shaggy black spruce trees. Dull yellow leaves cling to birch branches. Eight nervous ducks take to the sky, and a comical little brown bird darts from lily pad to lily pad on an earnest mission. This entertains me, and I momentarily forget that my toes are numb. Clumps of wet snow collect on the leatherleaf bushes at the water's edge. A beaver lodge, now a white mound, almost glows against the brown backdrop of the season's spent cattails.

Delicate yet hardy, these yellow lady's slippers are covered with morning dew.

A Country Bumpkin Visits St. Paul

Checking my mailbox one spring afternoon, I pulled out a large white envelope. The return address read: The State of Minnesota, Office of the Governor, St. Paul, Minnesota. When I saw where it was from, my lips automatically hardened into a tight sneer.

"What the hell do they want now?" I said aloud in a 40-below-zero voice.

Being self-employed, I am always leery of anything related to government. By the time I looked at the mail, all of my massage therapy clients were gone for the day. I was tired and ready to sit down. I just wanted a moment to collect my thoughts.

Already angry from imagining what the envelope might contain, I hastily ripped it open and was astonished. I took off my glasses and read the contents. Then I put my glasses back on and read the contents again. The curly, navy blue embossed words remained the same. The First Lady of Minnesota, Mary Anderson Pawlenty, was inviting me, the Kayak Lady, to a dinner for notable and accomplished girls and women from around the state. The dinner was to be hosted at the Governor's Residence, from 6:30 to 8:30 p.m., on Thursday, June 1, 2006.

The letter went on to say that the First Lady and her assistant, Anne Kitterman, had done some "highly unscientific" research and come up with the names of several Minnesota women and girls, ranging in age from 11 to 93, who had done, and were doing, extraordinary things professionally, through volunteer work, or both. The dinner would be held in honor of this wide array of females. The letter also said the dinner was not a political event. The First Lady assumed that many of us did not agree with her husband's political views, and that was fine because he was not invited. I appreciated how upfront she was. It never even crossed my mind that he would be there since he was not female.

"… I hastily ripped it open and was astonished. I took off my glasses and read the contents. Then I put my glasses back on and read the contents again."

What did cross my mind was how and why my name was on the invitation list. I thought I had received the invitation by mistake. Since it was well after five and too late in the day to call the RSVP number, I had to sleep on it. The next morning I called straight away.

The person on the line asked if I would be there, and I replied, "I would be delighted to join you."

It turned out that my name had come up in a newspaper story when Mrs. Pawlenty's assistant was doing Internet research about Minnesota women.

Upon learning of this prestigious event in my near future, my mother called to remind me to wear a bra, to not chew gum, and to please not belch at the table in front of the governor's wife.

With Mom's advice in mind, I did my best to be both proper and prompt. Horsethief Harry saw to it that I arrived safely in front of the stately three-story red brick mansion on Summit Avenue in St. Paul. With a quarter hour to spare before the arched black iron gate opened, he reminded me to breathe and to enjoy the evening. My tailored blouse, slipping bra straps, and heels kept reminding me that I was way out of my comfort zone. Fortunately, the Advil I swallowed on the four-hour drive down had kicked in. My familiar stomachache and nervous headache were gone.

A small crowd of well-dressed women had gathered. We were all taking photos in front of the locked gate when, exactly at 6:30 p.m., it automatically opened. In single file we stepped onto the red carpet that ran from the mansion to the sidewalk. I turned and waved goodbye to Harry.

From his station just inside the gate, a modern day butler checked my photo ID against the guest list. I moved toward the open door and suddenly realized I did not know how to address a governor's wife. Right then I decided I would just ask the next person I came to. An attractive brunette stood at the edge of the sidewalk near the front door. Smiling sweetly, she welcomed me to dinner, asked who I was, and gracefully shook my hand. Taking advantage of this one-on-one situation, I said, "Good evening. I am Mary the Kayak Lady from Grand Rapids. Please, can you tell me how I should address the First Lady of Minnesota?"

"Just call me Mary," the lovely lady whispered.

"Whoops!" I apologized, adding that I did not have a TV and did not know what she looked like.

First Lady Mary Anderson Pawlenty put her arm around me, gave me a hug, and said, "Tonight, we are all girlfriends, and we are here to have fun! And besides, I am never on TV anyway, so how would you know what I look like?"

Wow! Not only had I just met the First Lady, we had already become friends.

Mary invited me to look around the mansion and make myself at home. While visiting a few of the front rooms, I noticed the high ceilings, the polished hardwood floors, how dark the paneling was, how elegant and bright the chandeliers were, and that each room had a fireplace. It all had the feel of long ago. I liked being there. In one sitting room, I joined a woman who introduced herself as a news anchor for a metro television station. She had visited the governor's residence during the Jesse Ventura administration, and she wanted to see what was hanging above the fireplace in that particular room. A large portrait of Jesse Ventura dressed in armor had hung above the mantelpiece the last time she was there. We were both relieved to see the Minnesota state photograph, "Grace," hanging there instead.

"'Just call me Mary,' the lovely lady whispered."

"*Uffda!*" the anchorwoman proclaimed. "That sure looks better."

On this clear, mild evening, dinner was served buffet-style on the patio under a large canopy. The young and very attentive all-female wait staff offered a variety of beverages, including wine. Without any seating assignments, the event flowed freely, and the six tables set for eight filled. We casually lined up at the

Minnesota's state flower, the showy lady's slipper, grows in wet areas.

buffet table to serve ourselves wild greens, herbed wild rice pilaf, roasted sesame asparagus, grilled free-range chicken breast, and prime beef tenderloin.

Looking around, not wanting to miss any details, I spotted a party-sized Myers's Rum bottle sitting next to the large, grinning chef. He was the only male present, and he wore a traditional tall, white hat. As I passed by the jolly man, I asked if he would share some of that Myers's since it is my favorite rum. He laughed and said, "Yes! Just as soon as you clean your plate."

Dessert, itself, was a real show as the chef created two flaming treats: Bananas Foster (with the rum) and cherries jubilee. We were encouraged to sample both, and some of us did.

The First Lady joined my table, and after dinner she made a few remarks. She opened the floor to anyone who wanted to tell who they were and why they had been invited. First to speak was Morgan, an 11-year-old blind girl who had placed second in the National Braille Championship. The eldest dinner guest, 93-year-old Veda Ponikvar, founded the Chisholm Free Press in 1947. Still very much a stylish dresser and eloquent speaker, Veda told how she had beaten the odds in a man's world and successfully run the paper for 50 years. She was the most powerful speaker of the evening, and it seemed that she drew all of us in with

her words and mannerisms. I was inspired. Watching and listening, I felt that I wanted to be like her.

The Minnesota Teacher of the Year spoke, as did two 12-year-old girls who explained how they had started a nonprofit to raise 54 million dollars for the 54,000 schoolchildren affected by hurricanes Rita and Katrina.

When it was my turn, I told about falling through bogs and how observing moon shadows at an early age had taught me to seek out the subtle beauty in nature. At that point in my quest, I had paddled 755 lakes. The First Lady asked if I had paddled them alone.

"I sure try to," I answered.

On the way out the door, I thanked Mrs. Pawlenty for a fine dinner and invited her to join me kayaking. She answered, "I would like that very much. Perhaps next summer."

As we walked down the red-carpeted sidewalk to the street, the very jovial Minnesota Teacher of the Year, a woman comfortable in her own skin, wondered aloud, "Who would carpet their sidewalk?"

We giggled, hugged one another, and passed under the arched gate. It had been an enchanting evening.

A doe nurses her fawn alongside a country road.

 **fternoon of a Fawn**

One afternoon in late May I crossed
a clear-cut area on the way to Bog
Lake. Hearing twigs crack, I looked
up to see an alarmed doe springing
away. I trudged on. One more step
and her spotted baby would have
been under my foot. Curled in a
tight circle of rich chestnut, the silent
newborn was perfectly camouflaged
among last season's discarded
leaves. I froze. The fawn jumped up
and wobbly-walked a short distance.
We studied one another. Our magic
moment ended quickly as the suck-
ling found its strength and took tiny
leaps toward its mother.

Thick with ferns … the way ahead is not always easy.

Some I Paddle Topless

The first time it happened, it was a matter of survival. Honest, it really was.

When I began to paddle the lakes in Itasca County, I did not believe I would get to all of them. One of the entries on my 101-things-to-do-before-I-die list simply stated: Kayak 750 of the 1,007 lakes in Itasca County. At the onset, I figured that I probably would not paddle a lake if it looked too tricky to find or too difficult to reach. As I depleted the inventory of easy lakes that required no planning—public access lakes, lakes along the side of the road, or those that were a mere quarter of a mile down a wide trail—I began to experience growing pains. As the project advanced and I entered into the you-are-going-to-have-to-work-hard-for-this-lake era, I still had much to learn.

My first paddle on Pickerel Lake took place late on a calm, clear summer evening. Finding the tiny trickle of water that ran from Spruce to Pickerel was not a problem, but navigating it was. After fighting the narrowing creek for 15 feet, with cedar branches slapping my face and water too shallow to float the kayak, I gave up. Just like that, I gave up. But I did not stop thinking about going back.

Six summers and 451 lakes later, on a warm, sunny morning in early June, I tried again. On that trip across Pickerel Lake I was prepared, with both fireman boots and determination, to make the trek into Spruce Lake. Once again, locating the inlet from Spruce was easy. This time I did not give up when the paddling became impossible. Instead, I did the opposite. Without hesitation, I jumped out of the kayak and began dragging it over the soft carpet of green and red sphagnum moss. Bumping over clumps of fuzzy Labrador tea and past bright bunches of perky yellow marsh marigolds, I felt the sun's intensity on my shoulders and back.

Occasionally I had to lift the boat over a root or a rock. In some places the creek was muddy. In other spots the clear water was deep enough to go over the tops of my boots, and it did. I sloshed in muck. One time I moved forward while my left boot remained mired in the rich black goop. Wobbling and off balance, I watched my foot, with its dangling gray stocking, search for and find a landing place on a large speckled rock. The goofiness of it all made me laugh aloud. I was happy, felt strong, and remained undaunted. After all, the map showed that Spruce Lake was just behind Pickerel, and I believed it.

Squinting as I peered through the leaves and brush, I was relieved when I finally saw blue water on the other side of the tall cedar trees.

"I was happy, felt strong, and remained undaunted. After all, the map showed that Spruce Lake was just behind Pickerel, and I believed it."

By the time I reached the edge of Spruce Lake, I was hot and breathing rapidly—glowing in fact. Frogs and a handful of minnows played in the warm shallows. From experience, I knew it would be hard to identify the exact spot where I was standing because the pussy willows were thick. Having no pink ribbons to mark my exit route, I did the only practical thing I could think of. I simply slipped off my sleeveless pink T-shirt and threw it over the closest branch. I paddled the lake topless and instantly knew that I was onto something delightful. At first it seemed a little bit naughty, but that feeling soon dissolved into what felt very natural. None of the creatures I encountered—a great blue heron fishing along the water's edge, the family of ducks paddling nearby, or the red-brown deer watching from shore—seemed

High winds move the big trees. Thick reeds offer protection for a paddler.

bothered about my not wearing a shirt; nor was I. That was just the first of many topless paddles.

One afternoon in mid September when it was once again sunny and warm, I struggled to schlep the kayak through a tall stand of thick cattails into Seaman Lake, 12 murky acres occupied only by white water lilies and two old beaver huts. Although Seaman was a mere 200 feet from the road, I was out of breath and overheated by the time I got the boat into the water. To reward myself for the effort, I removed my top. Hearing a car roar by on the gravel road did not alarm me because the cattails created a bulky blind. No one could see the lake, let alone a topless kayaker.

A few years later, I decided to visit Four Town Lake. It was a calm, cloudless, and humid June morning— so quiet that not even the chickadees stirred. The thermometer read 86 degrees.

Earlier that spring, when the trees were bare of leaves, I found my way into the lake on a sloppy two-track trail. As usual, I tied pink ribbons at all of the forks in the trail to let me know where I had been.

On the day I returned, the mosquitoes and black flies were determined to taste my flesh. In an attempt to deter the flying pests, I put on long sleeves, long pants, a cap, and gloves. Although it sounds as if Four Town Lake might be in a populated area, it is not. I was alone out there, and I was completely

aware of it. Strapping the kayak onto its cart, I mustered up my courage, took a deep breath, and headed down the trail into the woods for the 25-minute hike to the water.

Anxious to see something familiar and reassuring, I hastened my stride and looked ahead for the pink ribbons. I did not see any. Instead, I saw and stepped on deer tracks, around bear tracks, and over wolf tracks. Earlier that week, a friend of mine who lives in the area told me that someone had seen a cougar up there. I was hoping the next tracks I encountered were not those of a large cat. I started to sing loudly, then whistle, and finally I resorted to praying. The noises did the trick. I encountered no wildlife, and I eventually found the pink ribbons.

Swatting at horseflies, I plowed through waist-high ferns, ducked under highbush cranberry branches, skirted around mud holes, and enjoyed the shade of large box elder trees as I passed under them.

By the time I came to the last Y, I sensed that there might be a faster way into the lake than I had previously found. Ignoring my pink marker, I followed what looked like a more heavily used trail that took me to a clearing by the water's edge. I stood by an overturned aluminum boat that looked as if it had seen use, but not recently. Believing that no one else would be venturing back to Four Town Lake that afternoon, I stripped, wrung out my sweat-drenched clothes, and draped them on the hot boat. But at the last minute I thought better of leaving them there to dry. I did not want an animal or the wind to move them. So I strapped my shirt, pants, socks, duck shoes, and gloves to the deck of the kayak. My moist cap went back on my damp head.

I really wanted to just jump in the lake to cool down and rinse off, but the pale brown water of Four Town Lake was not at all inviting. I shrugged my shoulders, climbed into the kayak, and quietly drifted alongside the cattails. From a well-hidden nest, a loon loudly announced its presence and flapped its way past me to a splashing finish. It dove and was out of sight. As my startled heart slowed to its pre-loon disturbance rate, my senses remained on high alert. From somewhere deep in the bog that surrounded most of the lake, I heard the slow and distinctive pump-er-wink, pump-er-wink call of an American Bittern (appropriately nicknamed *slough pump*).

Usually that curious booming call makes me smile, but it did not on that hot, still day. I was on edge. I may have felt vulnerable for one or more of several reasons: the sticky walk in, being without clothes, the startled loon, the soft bottom just four feet below me, or the loneliness of the lake. Whatever the cause of my uneasiness, I did not linger on Four Town any longer then it took me to paddle the shoreline, take the Secchi disk reading, and leave. Nothing distressing happened on my hurried trek out, but the closer I got to the truck, the more secure I felt.

Through the years I continued to paddle topless, but after Four Town Lake I never again paddled naked.

Canada geese rest on the shore of Cole Lake.

 ecret Spooners

The kayak hangs off my right shoulder
as I hike the portage trail from Little
Arm Lake over to Three Island Lake.
Along the way my foot disturbs a
decaying log and uncovers the day's
bonus. In the cool damp, two blue-
spotted salamanders are spooning.
So deep is my desire to become
part of their private world, I fall to
my hands and knees. When my eyes
have had their fill, and my nostrils
are satiated with their earthiness, I
bid them farewell and gently replace
their rotting roof.

Morning mist and morning sun reward an early start on Bowstring Lake.

And Now, for Your Listening Pleasure

Mom and Dad usually listened to the classical radio station when I was growing up. They shunned country western music as if it was something that might actually hurt their ears. The big kids who rode my school bus did not like country music either. They said only poor people dialed in to country stations. After hearing that, I decided to not like Johnny Cash or any yodeling yahoos.

Mom kept a small static-prone radio in the kitchen. She would tune in to *the local*, as she called it, wanting to hear current weather conditions or the news. If by chance Mom happened to turn the radio on early and *that racket*, as Dad called it, came wafting over the airwaves, I knew there might be hell to pay if the announcer did not hurry up and start reporting the temperature. Sometimes Dad just walked outside. About then I would develop a small stomachache.

When I was a teenager, Mom and Dad left me in charge of the resort when they headed to town to do the banking and eat lunch. As soon as their taillights were out of sight, I bolted over to Dad's stereo, found a rock and roll station, and turned up the sound. I knew how to be boss. One time, I forgot to return the dial to the classical station and to turn down the volume. You bet I heard about that lapse of responsible behavior! I tried to be more careful after that, but one afternoon when I was in a hurry to find my popular music station, the little string that pulled the tuner back and forth came off its track. Dad took the radio into town to be repaired and forbade me to touch his stereo after that.

As a college student I had my own stereo. I often cranked it up, but I never broke it. On my dorm floor I was introduced to a wide array of music including reggae, which sounded foreign and erotic.

Later on, it turned out that I confined most of my radio use to time when I was driving.

Many folks have asked what I listen to while I am kayaking. I do not listen to music when I paddle. Instead, I pay attention to nature and to the small, quiet, courageous voice inside me.

Driving to and from lakes is a different matter. Early on, I listened to folk, classical, rock, or the local community radio station, KAXE. My all-time favorite was tuning in to Minnesota Public Radio on Saturday afternoons for all of the funky talk programs and, of course, *A Prairie Home Companion*, hosted by Garrison Keillor. Garrison and I had a date every Saturday

evening for a few years.

It was when I started listening to country music that Garrison and I quit going steady. We did not have an official separation; it was just that the antenna broke off my truck. Even though I wanted to hear what Garrison had to say, I could not find a way to maintain our connection. The end of our relationship was much harder on me than on Garrison, as he never even knew we were dating.

"I do not listen to music when I paddle. Instead, I pay attention to nature and to the small, quiet, courageous voice inside me."

As the lakes became increasingly difficult to find, and I drove down more and more snowmobile trails, old logging roads, and two-track trails that led to nowhere, my red truck got more scratched up. It even took on a few dents. The third time the antenna fatally tangled with a low balsam branch, I decided not to replace it. I knew the red pony was not going to stop getting into tight spots in the woods, and that I would just have to take my chances on radio reception.

While traveling in the more remote areas of the county, I felt fortunate to pick up anything on the radio. That *anything* turned out to be a powerful 100,000-watt country station. We began keeping company, and after a while we became friends. I started recognizing tunes and began listening to the words carefully. The next thing I knew, I was singing along. There were a few songs I could barely tolerate, and of course there were some that had me sniffling and wiping my eyes.

"I knew the red pony was not going to stop getting into tight spots in the woods, and that I would just have to take my chances on radio reception."

Some afternoons when I drove around scouting for lakes, I found myself crying regardless of what was playing. Hearing a Mozart concerto reminded me of my deceased dad, and *Nights in White Satin* carried me back to a festive day at the Renaissance Fair with Gary before he and I were married. There were also times when tears came without the accompaniment of music, just because I felt frustrated, lonely,

or exhausted. Spotting a fragile fawn nursing at its mother's side or seeing the most perfect shade of red on a maple tree in autumn made me choke up and weep. Often I had no immediate clue why the tears gushed, I just let them flow.

Sometimes the tears knew more than I did. They taught me to sit with my pain, to feel my sorrow, and to identify my heartache. Tears do not lie when you are honest with yourself. I simply needed a safe space to release my tears, to hang them out to dry. Fortunately, some of them blew away on the summer breezes. Listening to country music helped me along because it reminded me that I was not alone in the sadness department.

I also learned that country music could be fun. Sometimes it even made me grin. One station in southeastern Arizona that I listened to when visiting my mom had a daily happy hour. Each afternoon the station selected a different upbeat country tune and then played it at the prescribed time. Mom and I tried to listen to the happy hour song together because the idea made us laugh. Other times we just took our chances and listened to whatever the station was broadcasting.

A few years ago Mom got very interested in a catchy country song with the words, "She left the suds in the bucket and the clothes hangin' out on the line." After we heard the tune a number of times, Mom began asking me what happened next.

"Had the woman just up and left, or what?" Mom wondered aloud.

I said I did not know because the song did not have a sequel. I told Mom she could make up any ending she wanted. If she did make up an ending, she never shared it with me. We all like a little drama in our lives from time to time; the source does not matter as much as the intrigue of the situation.

After a year and a half without an antenna, I was finally ready to try again. Big Brother Bob suggested installing a spring antenna which solved the breakage problem. It also allowed me to flip back and forth among a number of stations, and Garrison Keillor and I were able to resume our relationship. To this day I have one of the red pony's radio buttons pre-set to a country western station that I now listen to by choice.

appy Cluckers

Although we were 65 miles north of town in the middle of nowhere, Art Norton and I sensed we were not alone as we unloaded our gear. Suddenly, an incredibly clean chicken let loose a string of enthusiastic clucks and then jumped onto the deck of Art's kayak. Before we knew it, the rest of a small flock came running over and surrounded us. The chickens were cordial and escorted Art and me down to Little Dew Lake. When we returned to the landing they were there to greet us and walk us back up to the truck.

Late summer clouds are mirrored on peaceful Moosetrack Lake.

Do Your Dogs Bite?

Most lakes in Itasca County are either touched by or surrounded by public land, a factor that allowed me access to the water without having to cross private property. For the rest of the lakes it was necessary to ask permission or to trespass. All but a few of the property owners or caretakers I encountered were more than willing to give me support. When I knocked on a cabin door, I was looking for authorization to cross private property. Frequently I received more than I asked for—usually in favorable ways.

Many landowners simply gave directions and an approving nod. Others refilled my water bottle; or, if it was really hot, sent a can of cold soda along with me. Humanity's gracious side often came forth.

Late one cloudy and cool October afternoon, while driving in the northeast corner of the county, I pulled up to a garage near Spring Lake. The sweet smell of balsam boughs greeted me as I stuck my head inside the door to inquire about using the dock. I saw an industrious couple making holiday wreaths. They hoped to sell enough wreaths, they told me, to be able to take a cruise.

The wife's name was Mary, and she was pleased to have a visitor. Mary was very interested in having a kayak go around her lake. She even called her sister-in-law, who walked over, and both women cheered me on as I paddled. After I got off the water, the kind-faced and motherly Mary invited me into her kitchen where she served me a steaming bowl of homemade chicken dumpling soup. I ran into Mary years later, and we reminisced about the afternoon we met. She did not remember the soup, but did recall the excitement of having a kayak on Spring Lake. And yes, she said, they had sold enough wreaths and gone on a fine vacation that year.

On another occasion, a May evening paddle on Busties Lake, I needed to make a phone call. I did not own a cell phone at the time, so I drove over to the one home that was visible from the public landing. On the way to the front door I noticed an all-but-empty gallon wine jug on the woodpile. Half an inch of red wine remained in the bottom, and it was spotted with tiny black dots. Upon close examination, I saw dozens of once drunk—but now very dead—wood ticks that had finally quenched their thirst. After using the phone, I accepted the invitation from the helpful homeowner and gladly made my own contribution to the jug as I passed by.

Near the top of my accommodation-to-visitors list is Frank in the Suomi area. Not only did he help me launch my kayak on his lake, but while I was out paddling he made a call to his brother-in-law. When I returned, Frank guided me through the woods to the brother-in-law's remote lake. Years later I spoke at a Suomi Area Lake Association meeting and recounted the story. From the audience, Frank waved his hand, smiled, and humbly said, "That was me."

And then there was the jovial Sand Lake man who stood on the end of his dock one calm evening with a cocktail in hand. He invited me in for happy hour. I needed to get out of the kayak to stretch anyway, so I figured, "Why not?"

He and his wife offered spirited conversation and shared their tasty hors d'oeuvres. The sun had set when I took my leave carrying the rest of my gin and tonic in a paper cup. Sadly, I ended up pouring the potion out as I paddled. One-handed kayaking is difficult, let alone at dusk, and I still had to load the boat and find my way home.

Jack, on Jack Lake, caught me breaking the law. It would have been hard not to notice company once his dogs began barking and racing around the truck. There was no sneaking out of his yard after that. I had unhooked the red gate with the no trespassing sign attached to it and idled down the grassy drive. It was a Sunday evening, and I figured no one would be around. I was wrong. Immediately, I admitted I was trespassing, introduced myself, and handed the man a business card. Instead of calling the authorities or duct taping me to a lawn chair, the man smiled and explained that his name was Jack, but not the Jack for whom the lake was named. He went on to say that he had been picking lowbush cranberries that morning and might have crossed a few property lines in the process. We both laughed.

Jack offered a handful of the tangy berries. Soft and squishy, but still intact, the maroon-colored fruit had ripened the previous autumn and then spent the winter trapped in the bog under the snow. Jack gave details about how he enjoyed sprinkling the marble-sized cranberries on his cereal. Then, without any further fanfare or stories, he simply helped me unload the kayak and carry it to the water's edge. Jack gave me a heads up about the resident beaver that patrolled the lake, and with that said, returned to his log cabin. As it turned out, the most hassle I received on that escapade was from the tail-slapping beaver.

Over the years, I have considered the reasons why so many property owners were helpful. It may have been my small size, all of the favorable publicity I had received, or genuine interest in the project that eased the way. Or maybe people simply did not care

if I was on their lake as long as I was not fishing or misbehaving. Permission to paddle one lake pivoted on the point of whether or not I was going to drink beer while on the water. I gave the honest and correct answer, "No, I will not be drinking any beer anywhere today." With that, I was given the go-ahead.

"Jack gave me a heads up about the resident beaver that patrolled the lake, and with that said, returned to his log cabin. As it turned out, the most hassle I received on that escapade was from the tail-slapping beaver."

Only rarely was I turned down when I asked for the privilege to cross private property. It happened less than half a dozen times. On occasion there was no one on the premises to ask, but the "Keep out!" message still came across clearly.

Such was the case one time when I pulled into a narrow, tree-lined lane. Soon I spied a gatepost with a very special sign tacked to it. Someone had a sense

Water flies as a beaver's tail smacks the surface of DNR Lake #748.

of humor. The majority of the poster showed the back end of a caricaturized donkey. The very agile beast of burden had turned its tiny face around to reveal a mouth full of teeth. Above the donkey's head the sign read "KEEP YOUR," and below the donkey's very ample behind, complete with a wide crack, it said, "OUT!" I still kick myself for not snapping a photo of that one.

One memorable verbal refusal came from a tall man with an authoritative voice. "There is nothing on that little lake that you want," he announced as he handed back the Kayak Lady business card I had just given him.

I left, but the man's stern words motivated me to get back there to see what he might be hiding. I did not forget our conversation. Every time I drove north or south past his cabin, catching a glimpse of the water through the wall of pine trees, I made up stories about what he could be concealing.

Three years passed, and one autumn afternoon something told me to pull into that driveway and try again. The man of the house might have moved, or perhaps he had just mellowed. The gray-bearded fellow who answered my knock consented to let me paddle the secret lake. I saw nothing there that appeared suspicious, but I did not look very hard. By then, I was just glad to have had the opportunity to get on that lake.

Some days when I saw a no trespassing sign I turned around straight away. Other days I proceeded farther down the road until my gut told me to turn around. In my more brave moments, I just kept going.

Such were the conditions one bright July afternoon. Feeling bold, I headed down a driveway lined with orange and black private signs. Trees grew right up to the edge of the gravel roadway. I began to feel uneasy, but with no suitable spot to turn around, I continued on. That was in the early days before I had the red truck. At the time, I was driving a sleek midnight blue, two-door Saab coupe with the kayak strapped to the roof. It was quite a sight, and I thought I was pretty cool. Maybe that impressive rig fueled me forward.

The long and curvy drive went on and on. I started to wonder if I would ever arrive at a house. As I drove, I had plenty of time to consider that there might be a reason why some people chose to live at the end of the road. As I soon found out, those folks simply did not want visitors.

After what seemed like an eternity, an old, white farmhouse came into view. Taking a deep breath, I parked, opened the car door, and walked toward the house. I heard the growls before I saw the pair of lean, black dogs. I hastily retreated to the driver's seat. In a moment, the barking hounds were just outside my door. While backing the car around, I quickly rolled up the window. Then, out of the corner of my eye, I glimpsed a human figure moving on the screen porch.

Knowing the energetic watchdogs were in tight formation alongside the car, I gingerly unrolled the window just enough to shout through, but I did not get off the first word.

A husky female voice asked, "Whadda ya want?"

Although I could see water glistening in the sunshine down the hill, my reply was, "I was wondering if you could tell me where Monson Lake is?"

"There ain't no lake here," came the response from the porch.

Trying to make conversation, I asked, "Do your dogs bite?"

"They might," she said.

"Thank you," I shouted as I shifted the Saab into gear. Leaving a snaky dust trail, I sped away.

Eight years later I found a different route into Monson Lake. While on the water I caught sight of a roofline. I believe it belonged to the white farmhouse. I did not see or hear the dogs, nor the lady on the porch. Thinking back to that brief encounter, I smiled smugly to myself—satisfied to be paddling Monson Lake without having to ask permission from anyone.

Mirror, Mirror

The Schrocks' home was the closest to the road and Long Lake. Mrs. Schrock met me at the door. After chatting for a moment, she inquired if I would like to use the washroom. I thought this was odd, but figured I was her guest so I should accept her hospitality. When I washed my hands and looked in the mirror, it immediately became clear why I had been directed to the bathroom. On the drive up I had enjoyed a chocolate ice cream cone. Remnants of my fun had run off my lip, down my chin, and onto my neck.

A trumpeter swan and her eight cygnets swim through the water lilies.

Card Tricks and Cygnets

Just as Itasca County Commissioner Catherine McLynn and I clasped the last bungee cord securing the kayaks atop the red truck, it began to sprinkle. We left town anyway, eyes upturned to the gray sky. It was mid June so we expected anything and everything for weather. As the day unfolded, we got it.

Traveling with a public servant allows one the opportunity to do things one would not normally be inclined to do. As we drove out of town, Catherine casually mentioned that I should stop the truck ahead because she wanted to remove a dead deer from the highway. She did not need to tell me where to pull over. I had been seeing and smelling the bloated brown bundle for a few days as I passed by. I was not expected to help her, she matter-of-factly said, just to stop the red pony so she could do her chore. But wanting to be a responsible citizen, I joined her. We each grabbed a hind leg and without much effort quickly and efficiently relocated the doe from the shoulder to the ditch. Nature had already begun its composting process, so there was little weight. We scampered back across the pavement, cleaned our stinky hands with a couple of hand wipes, and sped away full of pride at being such helpful girls.

Hubbels' cozy cabin on Pine Lake was the next stop. All we intended to do was drop off a computer cord and say hello. As we pulled up, Martha was finishing a large omelet for John for Father's Day. Our timing was perfect. We walked in and sat down to share the tasty omelet, fresh handpicked strawberries, and homemade jam on dark bread toast. The wind howled while we sipped steaming mugs of tea and shared stories. Thunder shook the cabin. Lightning lit up the dark morning sky. More rain fell.

Catherine and I took our leave, vowing that by the time we reached the stop sign at Highway 38 we would make a decision. Either we would head north to find lakes, or we would retrace our path to town. Before we reached the highway, I remembered a bog-fringed lake I still needed to find and paddle. Since we were driving right past the turnoff, we decided to scout it out. Parking at the red gate, we saw a large brown cattail marsh off to the right. At the risk of getting wet, we ventured behind the locked gate and soon discovered that the little unnamed lake I was hunting for sat in the center of the bog. It would be wet work dragging my kayak out there, so we decided to save the trip for another day.

"The wind howled while we sipped steaming mugs of tea and shared stories. Thunder shook the cabin. Lightning lit up the dark morning sky. More rain fell."

By then the rain had slowed to a few sprinkles. Wanting to stretch our legs and walk off Martha's hearty breakfast, we set off down the two-track driveway. Along the way we encountered a painted turtle that appeared to be laying eggs. The eyes stared up at us as we walked by, but the turtle did not move. We looked closely and discovered that the turtle was dead—a mere shell with nothing inside.

It seemed as if we hiked forever, but in reality it was only about 20 minutes. Blue water appeared on our right, and soon after more water appeared on our left. Unsure of where we were, I started guessing. My best guess was Jack the Horse Lake as there were no cabins and the water covered a rather large area. Before long we smelled wood smoke. Catherine, in true county commissioner style, started calling out, "Good morning! Hello?"

All we saw was a car with California plates parked

A pair of trumpeter swans sits on melting ice during spring breakup on Round Lake.

by a white cabin that probably dated back to before either of us was born. The smoke smelled friendly, reminding me of my days growing up in a little cabin heated by wood. I marched up to the door and gave it a hearty knock.

A solid, "Good morning!" boomed back.

We walked in and were greeted by a jolly man with a full white beard. He asked if we wanted some coffee. We declined, but were grateful for the opportunity to warm ourselves by the barrel stove.

Doug, our host, explained that we were on the ridge between Big Dick and Little Dick Lakes. He said his family had owned the lovely piece of property for many, many years. He and his siblings split expenses and vacation time there.

It was difficult for the three of us of to keep straight faces when talking about the Dick Lakes. Finally, Doug explained that the name had come from the days when men worked in lumber camps. The lumberjacks enjoyed playing cards after working all day in the woods. If someone was dealt a rotten hand while playing poker, he said he had been given the "little dick." When the hand was really rotten, he had been dealt the "big dick."

Doug's story about cards tied right in with his next utterance. "I want to humor you girls for a minute," he said.

Pulling out an ordinary deck of cards, he asked for complete silence, saying he needed to concentrate very hard. Then he shuffled the deck, drew out a card without looking at its face, and placed it face down on the table. Lips silently moving, he walked his way through the deck one card at a time until he had looked at each card face. Then, without any fanfare, he announced that the unturned card was a nine. Indeed, it was.

When pressed for details about how he had chosen the right card, Doug would only say, "Careful counting."

On that note we bid our new friend goodbye, but only after we had been given permission to cross his land and paddle the bog lake on a drier day. We were intrigued by the card demonstration. Although we had not learned the trick, we did have something more to think about and discuss the rest of the day.

By the time we had hiked back to the truck, the rain had stopped. At Highway 38, we headed north. We drove for the better part of an hour, sometimes in sunshine and sometimes in thunderstorms. Following a road that narrowed at each intersection, we found what we were looking for and ended up portaging into a small unnamed lake in northeastern Itasca County.

After paddling through a narrow channel filled with cattails, we found ourselves peacefully gliding along the shoreline. There was plenty to see and hear.

White water lilies dotted the lake's surface while blue flag iris added color to the marshy shoreline. Three low-flying vultures soared overhead. Perhaps the birds saw the kayakers and were thinking "fresh meat." A loon let out an alarm call as a bald eagle flew down the center of the lake. As we floated past the tall marsh grass we spotted the eagle's mate sitting in a dead pine at the far end of the lake. Just then the loon pair came into view. The loons swam close to each other and then dove out of sight.

As Catherine paddled ahead toward the mouth of the creek, we heard an excited honking-trumpeting sound. At first I thought it was panicky geese sounding off, but I quickly realized it was not geese making the noise at all. By then Catherine had cleared the outlet and was in open water. I saw the two unmistakable long white necks of trumpeter swans. I raised the camera and began snapping photos as quickly as the camera could record them.

Sighting swans is not as rare as it used to be, but the next sight was unusual. Following one parent downstream were eight fluffy, whitish-gray swan babies known as cygnets. The other mature swan headed in the opposite direction from the family. He had become quite agitated, as one might imagine a protective parent would. The powerful bird stretched out his wings and ran atop the water—letting out a deafening distress call and flapping his enormous

wings the whole while. The swan never lifted more than a foot or two off the water, his black webbed feet leaving puddle rings in his wake. The white blur was headed toward Catherine.

Sensing potential danger I shouted, "We need to get out of here! We need to get out of here now!"

Catherine was already beating a hasty retreat to the far shore.

Sensing potential danger I shouted, "We need to get out of here! We need to get out of here now!"

Not sure where the crazed swan might head next, I was instantly concerned for my own safety. His outstretched neck was longer than my arm and many, many times stronger and more flexible. Knowing I was no match for a full-grown trumpeter swan with issues, particularly on its own territory, I put the camera down and picked up my paddle. If I needed to protect myself, I figured, I would unsnap my six-foot-long paddle and use one half as a baseball bat—that was if I had the good fortune to get in the first swing. It is always good to have a plan. Fortunately, I did not need to protect myself. In his no nonsense way, the swan had escorted us away from his family.

When the swan was satisfied that we were leaving, it tucked its long wings back in place and swam the perimeter of the lake. The bird stopped making its alarmed call when we were out of sight.

On my way off the lake I paddled by a tiny boggy island. Two spotted olive-brown loon eggs sat securely on their nest at the water's edge. The unborn chicks were silent witnesses to all of the excitement, quietly preparing for their own adventures.

Reprimanded

Slowly paddling the weedy shoreline of Edmond Lake, I suddenly had a very feisty and loud green heron mama fluttering in my face. She commanded and received my full attention, and that is when I noticed my right shoulder was about to collide with her nest made of small sticks. The basket nest hung from the end of a willow branch about 18 inches above the water. Four pale-green eggs rested inside. What really caught me off guard was the red-winged blackbird that joined its green heron neighbor—not only scolding me loudly in his own language, but also repeatedly flying at my head. I apologized to both birds for my carelessness and immediately paddled away.

Trees create a keyhole view of beautiful Mystery Lake.

Secret Lake M

One day in mid June I went scouting for a suitable route into Secret Lake M. The topographic map showed a U.S. Forest Service road running north of the lake. Thinking there might be an offshoot leading to the water, I started down the shady Forest Service lane.

My ability to find a lake had not been tested very much, nor had my Baja-style driving skills, but I was optimistic. Glancing at the odometer after navigating the rough track for a time, I saw I had already traveled nine-tenths of a mile. I began to wonder just how far I might be going when the right side of the truck dropped into a rutted mud hole and stopped. I nonchalantly put the truck in four-wheel drive high and stepped on the gas. The motor roared. Water flew. Sodden gray clay came in through the open window. Mud splattered the windshield. The truck did not budge.

"No problem," I thought. I still had four-wheel drive low to try. I hit the gas again. The motor roared louder. Water flew farther. More sodden gray clay came in through the open window, this time hitting my shoulder and neck. The only thing that changed was the amount of mud on the windshield. I was astonished. I could not see in front of me, but I could clearly see that I was in trouble.

"The only thing that changed was the amount of mud on the windshield."

After pushing the door open, I jumped away from the truck and quickly assessed the situation. The red pony sat tilted at a sickening angle with the passenger side tires buried halfway in gumbo. Figuring that it was time for heavy-duty action, I dug behind the seat for my come-along, the modern day version of a block-and-tackle. Big Brother Bob had given me the Power-Pull the previous Christmas. Fortunately he had thrown a short rope into the box. Unfortunately, we had not run through a practice session with the device. I found the instructions and read, and then reread, how to attach what end to where and what to do with auxiliary rope if needed.

"Pray as if everything depends on God, and act as if everything depends on me," I chanted aloud in a vain attempt to calm myself.

Doing my best to slow down and think things through, I tried to imagine what Bob would do under the circumstances. First, I decided, he would locate a sturdy tree for the come-along cable to go around.

I understood enough to know that the tree and the trailer hitch ball on the back of the truck had to be in close proximity. I spied a 10-inch maple. While setting up the cable, I quickly found out that the maple was four-and-one-half-feet out of reach. I sure was glad Bob had thought to put in the extra rope because I was going to need it. What I really needed, I thought, was for him to magically appear and help me, but that fantasy evaporated as quickly as it formed. Getting back to reality, I looped the cable around the tree, secured the rope to the cable, and fastened the hook to the trailer hitch ball. I had a hunch that some element critical to the whole operation was missing. Quite frankly, I had no clue what that component might be; but for good measure I pretended that I knew and allowed for it. Really unsure of what else to do, I began cranking the come-along handle.

The next few moments did not bring the results I wanted. The truck did not creep toward me. Instead, the tree did. Creak! Crack! Immediately I stopped cranking. The maple tree I had chosen was a dead one. It was the tree standing next to it that sported the full leafy branches. As a tomboy who had grown up in the woods, I felt foolish. I did not crack a smile or laugh, but cursed curtly. Before setting up the cable and rope the second time, I made certain that I found and used a living tree. Angry and fueled by adrenaline, I cranked so fast, so hard, and so wildly, that sweat ran down my back and blood covered my nicked-up fingers. Still, the truck did not stir. The cable and rope had become taut enough to walk on. But I did not try it. I was more than disheartened by the task at hand. I felt I had run into a stone wall.

"As a tomboy who had grown up in the woods, I felt foolish. I did not crack a smile or laugh, but cursed curtly."

Wondering what could possibly be wrong this time, I bolted over to the truck to investigate. Then it hit me. I had left the truck in park. No wonder it had not moved. I got in, started it up, shifted into neutral, got out, and jammed a stick into the mud by the back bumper to mark my progress. Then I resumed cranking. Inch-by-inch, the tires crawled toward me. If putting the truck in neutral worked so well, I decided that shifting it into reverse would work even better. And it did.

It took an hour and a quarter, but the truck was free; and I had learned the basics of how to employ a come-along. I did not explore any more that day, but I did not go straight home either. Doing the only thing I knew that would help, I drove to the closest store and had a double scoop of chocolate ice cream. When I unloaded the kayak that evening, I found mud on top of it. When I showered that night, I found mud in my hair. The next morning I took the red pony to the car wash.

From then on, whenever I approached a mud puddle—small or large—I parked the truck and investigated before I drove forward. I would find a strong stick and poke it in the water to determine how deep the puddle was and what type bottom it had. I also learned to put the truck in four-wheel drive long before I needed it. Of course I never forgot about getting mired in the mud that day, or that I had not found Secret Lake M.

Five more summers came and went. While studying the *Itasca County Land Atlas and Plat Book* one evening, I paused on the page that included Secret Lake M. Looking carefully, I recognized the name on the land next to it. After a few phone calls, I was granted permission to cross private property to access the lake.

Horsethief Harry and I took advantage of the invitation and drove over one colorful autumn day. A road—a very passable road—led right to the creek

A great blue heron hunts for a meal in the shallows of Bowstring Lake.

that flowed out of Secret Lake M.

The water level where we found a clear spot to launch our kayaks was a mere six inches deep. Tall brown cattails, both thick and stocky, impeded our progress. Once we got away from them, the creek became clogged with wild rice. It worked better to shove the kayaks along than it did to paddle. It was true grunt work. Dislodged kernels of rice landed with hard plinks on and in our boats. Naturally, the closer we got to the lake, the deeper the water became. But everything is relative. The lake topped out at three and a half feet deep. The water was crystal clear, revealing a clean bottom of powdery soft slate-colored silt. Thinking back to our phone conversation, I recalled the landowner mentioning something about pounding in posts for a duck blind back there. When the poles had sunk to a depth of 16 feet, he quit driving them down and trusted that they were in far enough. Perhaps Secret Lake M did not have a bottom. I hoped we would not find out.

Once on the lake, Harry spotted a school of tiny wiggling bullheads. There must have been 100 black whale-shaped bodies that looked to be mainly skull. We wondered if bullheads were smarter than other fish since they appeared to have such large cranial areas. Outside of the baby bullheads, we saw nothing noteworthy.

Even if I had been able to get past the monster mud hole on my first attempt to find Secret Lake M, I would have had trouble launching the boat without wearing water wings. The lake was surrounded by a wetland with a thick border of trees just beyond it. We saw nary an opening to allow access to the water. Nor did we see anything that resembled a trail next to the lake.

Harry paddled ahead, poking around a small wild rice and cattail nook. Slowly I glided along, staring down at the weatherworn and bug-bitten lily pads. Their season was over. A melancholy moment washed over me. I was getting closer to the end of my mission to kayak each of the lakes in the county. Along with the melancholy, I felt a sense of victory about finally reaching Secret Lake M. There were still some very challenging waters to find and paddle, but I was confident I would complete the task. By then I had found and kayaked 863 lakes. I had acquired the skills and patience to find a lake—more often than not—when I set my sights on doing so. Along the way I had learned to ask for and accept the help of others. Finding Secret Lake M proved that it pays to be persistent.

It is too muddy to use the cart, so it is strapped to the kayak for the journey into Rip Lake.

ail Yes!

My concern about being out in the rain instantly vanished as hail began striking and bouncing off the kayak and my head. I removed my glasses and pulled my cap down over my face in an attempt to keep dry. Drenched and shivering, I wanted to get off Rip Lake and under a tree as soon as possible. The red pony was an hour and a half away. I knew that Catherine and I would have to drag the kayak back through shin-deep ruts in oozy, black, boot-sucking muck. But schlepping through mud seemed like a minor problem compared to what was really on my mind. I wondered if that Frisbee-sized snapping turtle we had encountered submerged in the first mud puddle back by the truck was lying in wait for our return.

Orange leaves contrast with blue sky near Beavertail Lake.

Rice Lake Floatplane

I believed there would be a fly-in adventure some day. I just did not know which lake it would be, with whom, or when. As the lakes became more challenging to reach, it seemed more and more likely that I would need the help of a skilled pilot and a floatplane.

It was not unusual for people to ask, "So, how will you get to such and such lake? Will someone drop you in from a helicopter and haul you back up with a rope?"

The questions were usually followed by nervous, teasing laughter, and sometimes the questioner added, "Maybe they will just leave you there."

Jerry Snustad, also known as Sky King, and I were used to flying together because we had spent half a summer soaring from lake to lake offering flight seeing float-plane rides to resort guests. We flew in his 1947 Piper PA-12 Super Cruiser and followed a route Monday through Thursday, visiting four or five area resorts and campgrounds each day. Sometimes the workdays were short and we spent a fair amount of the outing eating ice cream, sampling hot homemade caramel rolls, and enjoying burgers at the establishments we visited. Other days, we barely had a moment to eat. After 12 hours of touring lakes, we would drag back to Jerry's house to clean up the plane and make a plan for our next trip. Once operating expenses were met, we split the profits.

It seemed like a bonus to go home with money in my pocket after an entire day of flying. Spending time in the plane was exciting. I liked meeting people, and selling vacationers on the idea of taking a floatplane ride energized me. Flights around the county also gave me chances to look for trails leading into hidden lakes. I was living my dream job—having fun and getting paid for it. I was thrilled.

From my flight seeing days, I had gained a rough idea about how much water surface area a small floatplane needed to land and take off. Somewhere along the line I began keeping a mental list of contenders for arrive-from-the-air-only lakes. After flying over Rice Lake a number of times, I knew it was a likely candidate.

The winter after I was Jerry's sidekick, I asked Big Brother Bob if he knew anything about Rice Lake.

"I've been out there a couple of times and can show you where it is," he said.

One bright January morning I climbed on the back of Bob's snowmobile. In a cloud of exhaust we left his house and roared west across Deer Lake at full throttle. I hung on tightly as we bumped along for a considerable time on a narrow trail through a dense black spruce swamp. Eventually we stopped on a large, flat, open area, and Bob shut off the machine. I saw the hump of a snow-covered beaver lodge and knew we were on a frozen lake.

My brother announced, "Here you are on Rice Lake. This might be the closest you ever get to paddling it."

Looking around, I distinctly remember studying the terrain and thinking that he was probably right. But I never gave up on the idea of returning with a kayak.

"But I never gave up on the idea of returning with a kayak."

Gathering information for a potential route into Rice Lake was frustrating. I left phone messages for a number of folks in that neighborhood, but got no responses. A friend who had hunted ducks in the area cautioned that it would take an extended and very wet hike to reach the lake. He had tried to go in by boat, but turned back because fallen trees made the small creek impassable. After studying the map some more and exploring the surrounding area on foot, I concluded that the most favorable way to transport a kayak to Rice Lake was via Jerry's floatplane.

Deciding which kayak to take along took much less time and effort than the rest of the planning. Straightaway, we decided against strapping my wooden craft to the pontoons. Jerry assured me it could be done, but securing the kayak to the floatplane would be more trouble then it was worth. There was too much potential for something to go wrong.

My boat problems were solved when a helpful friend, Kim the Buddhist, offered to let me use her inflatable kayak, a blue and gray mass of heavy-duty plastic. Rice Lake turned out to be the only lake I paddled where I did not use my own wooden kayak.

Kim and I figured a dry run with the plastic kayak would be prudent. I did not want to arrive at Rice Lake missing a critical piece of the hand pump or not knowing how to use it. My goal was to be efficient so I would not waste Jerry's time.

I began the practice session by pumping air into Kim's kayak until I thought it was full enough to float successfully. Then I strapped it to a kayak cart and pushed it down the hill to Ice Lake for a practice paddle.

The kayak and I would have flunked a DWI test.

"The kayak and I would have flunked a DWI test."

We were a sorry team, unable to walk or paddle in a straight line. But the craft floated, and I stayed relatively dry. Confident that I could sufficiently inflate and paddle the kayak, I loaded it back on the cart and made the return trip up the sloped street to my garage. Out of breath from the effort, I proceeded to wipe down the wet boat. Deflating it was harder than I had imagined. My lame attempts to push the air out with my hands and arms did little, so I finally ended up rolling my body over the clammy plastic to flatten it. I worked up a sweat folding the kayak into the most compact pile possible. By the time I finished, my clothes were thoroughly wet; but Kim's kayak and I were ready for Rice Lake.

Horsethief Harry thought the best way to prepare for the fly-in adventure would be to keep everything as authentic as possible. He grinned as he suggested that I turn my trash can on its side, stand on it, and pretend I was on the floatplane pontoon. That way, he said, I could get a feel for what it would be like to balance on a narrow platform while inflating and deflating the kayak.

There was plenty of free advice from other sources too. In fact, nearly everyone I spoke to about flying into Rice Lake offered counsel. There is nothing like an unusual event to pique people's interest and ignite their curiosity.

At long last, the evening for takeoff arrived, and I met Jerry at the Grand Rapids-Itasca County Airport on the shore of Lily Lake. The plane was already in the water when I drove up. Jerry suggested I load my gear while he went back to the hangar with the tug he had used to move the plane.

Staggering down to the wooden dock from my truck, I half carried, half dragged the deflated kayak toward the plane. I kept hoping that none of the dangling ropes would catch on anything and send the whole package into the drink. The plan was to get the folded kayak and all of my gear—paddle, Secchi disk, sponges, hand pump, and water bottle—stuffed into the luggage space behind my seat. To save room and insure I would not forget it, I wore my life jacket.

After a few well-chosen expletives and a little elbow grease, all components were jammed in place. Jerry slid into the pilot's seat. He reached back and handed me a headset. With the doors open for ventilation to cool off the snug and stuffy cockpit, he started the engine. We taxied to the far end of Lily Lake and slammed the doors. Hoping it was not too calm, too hot, or too humid to lift off, he gave it onion. We took off in a spray of water and headed northwest over Grand Rapids as the evening sun played hide-and-seek with slate gray clouds. It was the summer solstice. Although it is normally light until after 10 on the longest day of the year, the cloud cover warned that darkness would come early.

Fishermen waved at the red and white plane as we cruised low over Bass Lake. We traveled straight down the lake and buzzed Back O' the Moon Resort where I had grown up. Gaining altitude, we passed over Deer Lake and continued about five miles farther. I snapped photos during the whole ride. Soon we were circling a flat green sphere of water—little wonder that Rice Lake is also called Round Lake. It had clearly been a good idea to fly in; the expansive black spruce swamp surrounding Rice Lake was thick.

Jerry made a smooth landing, shut off the engine, and the plane coasted to a stop. Wasting no time, I wrestled the crumpled kayak out of the back. It was easy to unfold and flop over the pontoon. Jerry held the hose nozzle in place while I powered the hand pump. It was helpful that the pontoon was wider and flatter than I recalled. Neither Jerry nor I wanted to fall into Rice Lake's warm, brown water.

Once in the kayak, I paddled a bit and was surprised that I saw no wild rice growing. One lonely loon kept its distance. Both sky and water were glittery gray. The lake was large enough that it could have taken a while to paddle, but I did not explore the entire shoreline as was my usual practice. It was a stretch, in fact, to call it *shore*. A curved line of green, wet bog was all that separated the water from the trees.

Rice Lake was still and quiet that evening. The lake is a game reserve, but if there was any game other than the single loon in the area, it was quite reserved and did not make an appearance.

Jerry stood on the pontoon wearing a boyish smirk.

"Don't get any ideas!" I called out.

"Like leaving early?" he asked, his grin echoing the remarks of many who had joked about the idea of flying into a lake.

I lowered the Secchi disk over the side of the kayak and it quickly disappeared into the mucky lake bottom. The water was a mere five feet deep with only three and one half feet of water clarity. With that information obtained, it was time to paddle back to the plane and deflate the kayak. I was not looking forward to hugging the slippery serpent of wetness while trying to stay upright and dry on the pontoon, but Jerry assisted with the process and we soon had the kayak ready to stow.

While Jerry prepared for takeoff, I wrestled the dripping pile of plastic and assorted gear back into its confining cubbyhole. After some effort, every-

thing was strapped in place. The plane lifted off the smooth steel-colored lake and circled up, up, up.

I pressed my nose to the window, not wanting to miss a thing. Whisking along just above the tree-tops made it easy to pick out landmarks. Instantly, I recognized the mighty oak standing alone on one of the tiny islands as we crossed Big Green Lake. My thoughts flashed back to the afternoon I was there. Much water had dripped off my paddle since then. A decade had come and gone. Both the oak and I had weathered many storms. Seeing the tree gave me confidence and reminded me that I also stand strong on my own.

A stream of sunlight found a hole in the cloud cover and shot through. The sunbeam fell on an orange doe as she stepped out of the rich green woods to drink at the edge of a small pothole. Jerry and I simultaneously pointed and tapped the glass as we spotted her. The doe looked up. She was more curious than alarmed. Glimpsing the graceful doe was a gift, one that my memory unwraps again and again.

As we neared Grand Rapids, we saw more familiar sights. We glided above Shoal Lake, a gravel pit, McKinney Lake, the arena, Ice Lake, and over town. The sun was just beginning to set as the plane touched down again on Lily Lake.

Many interesting floaters, including this spike rush, inhabit the surface of Dead Horse Lake.

The Lake That Was

A little after midnight, when the woods were dark and quiet, Miller Lake made an escape. It did not sneak out as a teenager with watchful parents might; it went with a thunderous roar. Miller Lake has not been seen nor heard from since; and it may never return.

In July of 1993, a weak spot on the west side of Miller Lake gave way. The water and its assorted contents carved a wide gash down the hill and flowed into Amen Lake. Just a few weeks later, I had my first opportunity to visit the Miller Lake site. At that time, I had not paddled a kayak let alone thought of owning one. I thought canoes were king in those days.

A friend who lives on Amen Lake invited Gary and me out and loaned us a boat so we could cross the lake and see the destruction. Gary and I motored along the shore and found a secure spot to land. We explored the rest of the way on foot. Ripped and raw, the gaping gorge left in the wake of Miller Lake was unlike anything I had seen before. I could almost feel the powerful force of the released water.

We made our way up the hill, climbing over and under uprooted trees, maneuvering around rocks, and avoiding the slapping boughs of brush. Loose sand made it difficult to get a firm foothold. It was not easy going, and we were soon short of breath. When we finally arrived at the top of the gorge, we stood by what looked to be a broken beaver dam. All that remained were a half dozen jagged timbers forced apart and pointing away from the lake they once held in place. Where the lake had been, there was a shallow bowl of brown-black mud with a small wading pool of murky water in the middle.

When I was growing up on Bass Lake I often wondered what it would be like if all of the water drained out. When I mentioned this idea to my dad, he was horrified by the thought.

"Why would anyone want to drain such a beautiful lake?" he asked. "How would we make a living? No one would want to stay in a cabin on a big mud hole."

I imagined that removing the water would reveal outboard motors, anchors, eyeglasses, clothing, rods and reels, lures, landing nets, old docks, rotten boats, ice-fishing houses, or any number of surprises. But Miller Lake was not large enough, nor was it easy enough to access, to have such big-ticket items resting on its muddy bottom.

There was no loot. Although the site was intriguing just because it seemed unnatural, looking at a lake bottom was not as exciting as I expected. I had hoped for a glimpse at one of Mother Nature's precious secrets—the mysterious and confidential holdings of a lake—but I was disappointed. In its hurried escape, Miller Lake had taken along anything that might have been odd or difficult to explain. All that remained were a few orphaned deadheads anchored in the muck.

Through the years many have considered what happened at Miller Lake. Local residents reported hearing a loud roar like that of a tornado, only there had been no wind that night. A few thought something had exploded. Others said they heard what sounded like a freight train. By the light of day, it was apparent something bizarre had taken place. Overnight the water level on Amen Lake had come up a foot and a half. Several small floating bog islands made the lake their new home, and the once clear water had become murky. It took two or three years before the water was transparent again.

"By the light of day, it was apparent something bizarre had taken place."

In a foreshadowing of its ultimate escape, Miller Lake had split on the same side 11 years earlier. Most of the lake's contents had spilled out then. Neither Department of Natural Resources experts nor locals have been able to conclude what caused the eventual end of the lake. Theories fall into two categories: It may have been a buildup of water pressure that caused the beaver dam to blow, or it might have been erosion of sandy subsoil that weakened the site from underneath. It is possible that both contributed on the night that the small stream between Miller and Amen became a 65-foot-deep gully.

In the autumn of 1999, with my kayak in tow, I hiked in for a second look at Miller Lake. The water level remained about the same as it had been on my first visit. I did not think it was worth putting the kayak in to paddle such a puddle. Little did I know, that would be my last chance to kayak on what was left of Miller Lake.

In September of 2006, Horsethief Harry and I visited the Miller Lake site. Harry wanted to see the lakebed firsthand. The little pool of water had been transformed into a nearly dry, low-lying area of waving grass. Small clusters of cattails surrounded a slow trickle of water. The water wove a course toward the non-existent beaver dam, but disappeared before it reached its destination. Standing in the shallow bowl of the lake basin, we turned around to take it all in.

Above our heads, resting on the sloping shoreline of days gone by, was the sunbaked gray wood of an abandoned beaver lodge. Waist-high thistles grew around and on it. Soon, it too would disappear.

We continued though the middle of what had been the bottom of the lake. The closer we came to the remnants of the beaver dam, the faster we walked. We were eager to see what might still be in place. The rugged old timbers were as I remembered them; just a V-shaped slot remained. It was easy to imagine a waterfall running between the weathered logs now that the opening was bone dry. When the dam was intact, it most likely resembled many of the beaver dams we had encountered while kayaking. Harry and I agreed it would be very bad luck to be standing on such a dam when it gave way.

Red, orange and yellow autumn leaves offered a warm and welcome splash of color as we slowly traversed the curvy gorge that resembled a steep-sided gravel pit. The area felt safe and protected. In a modern-art sort of way, it was pretty. Hints of the story remained everywhere, yet new stories were in the making. Tracks from feet that frequented the sandy ravine were all over. Human prints mixed with those of grouse, deer, and bear. An assortment of wild and domestic canines had also come to investigate or, more likely, forage for a meal.

Although the landscape had dramatically changed as

a result of the two washouts, Mother Nature, in her usual way, was adapting well. She had been busy. A displaced strip of earth from the initial washout, that was at first a marshy sand beach, now was thick with scrub trees.

By the time the number of lakes left to kayak dwindled to fewer than 50, I decided to give Miller Lake one more try. From my previous visits, I knew the most efficient way in was by paddling across neighboring Little Horn Lake and then portaging the remainder of the way. On a perfectly calm and sunny afternoon in August of 2009 I did just that.

Since it had been a wet summer, I hoped to find a marginal amount of water for the kayak. Before I stepped off the old logging road to crash through a narrow bit of woods leading toward Miller Lake's former shoreline, I set the kayak down in the shade. Catching my breath, I paused for a moment, speculating as to whether or not I would find water.

I moved forward only to be snagged by shoulder-high raspberry bushes heavy with ripe berries. Apparently the old lake bottom was fertile. With no trees to crowd out or shade the bushes, they had simply gone wild and multiplied. The thorny bushes pulled at my sleeveless top, ripped my pants, and tore my skin. I gave up walking and gave in to gorging myself on the abundant sweet berries. It was a tasty reward for my efforts. There was no water, and I did not see remnants of the old beaver lodge that day.

Miller Lake is one lake I did not paddle on my quest—but it was not for lack of trying. Timing can be everything. Mine was off by a decade.

ut on a Limb

Craig Simon and I paddled Arrowhead Lake in mid November. Overhead, a male bald eagle shrieked as he approached his mate. Perched on a branch in a tree at the water's edge, she returned his call. He swooped in and landed beside her. They sat together quietly for a few moments. Then he moved behind her on the branch, flapping his wings the whole time. Bending her white head down and forward, she tipped her tail up to accommodate their mating activity. Within a few seconds, the male moved back beside his partner. They sat peacefully for a few minutes, and then he flew down the lake and out of sight.

Outdoor experts attribute reversed-season mating to a phenomenon called photoperiodism—a reaction to the amount of daylight

Water lilies create a pleasant place to rest on Ralph's Lake.

The Winds of Change

When gas prices reached nearly four dollars a gallon, I decided to reduce my driving speed to save resources. As a result, I began to see things I had not taken in before. Although I had traveled up and down the Scenic Highway dozens of times, I had never noticed a particular narrow, grassy pull-in. I stopped one day to investigate and found a well-worn path that led down a short slope to a lush pitcher plant bog. Beyond the bog was a tiny lake. My eyes had caught the glimmer of sunlight reflecting off that little body of water many times, but I had never taken time to explore a route into the hidden jewel.

Two weeks later I returned with my friend Judy. We carried our kayaks down to the bog and across a submerged boardwalk to the lake.

"The whole bog bounces when you walk across it!" Judy exclaimed.

Indeed, the Labrador tea plants, spilling over with slightly scented white flowers, jiggled whenever we took a step; and the fresh maroon and green pitcher plant flowers bounced on their spindly stocks. Water covered our feet as we crouched to study the dark green, veined leaves of bunchberry. Taking time to look carefully, we noted that its nickel-sized white flower petals were slightly stiff, resembling crisp cotton sheets sun-dried on a clothesline.

A need to stand up, accompanied by a glimpse of the dark blue water of the unnamed lake, reminded us of our mission. We continued our trip and launched our kayaks when we reached the edge of the bog. From the opposite shore, mature red pines welcomed us.

> "Taking time to look carefully, we noted that its nickel-sized white flower petals were slightly stiff, resembling crisp cotton sheets sun-dried on a clothesline."

Aside from the disturbance created by our kayaks and paddles, the lake did not have a ripple. Cumulonimbus clouds built overhead and created grand reflections of white and gray on the water's surface. Softly mirrored along the shore were watercolor images of pastel green tamaracks. As I slowly paddled, my eyes scanned the bog and took in its diverse colors and textures.

I caught a hint of pink and paddled backward to discover a family of four stemless lady's slippers standing together. The delicate moccasin flowers hung shyly above the mossy bog floor. Plainer in color than the showy and yellow lady's slippers, the stemless lady's slippers also have less foliage than their orchid cousins. We marveled at our find, and then bid our new flower friends farewell before resuming our tour.

Before we left the lake, Mother Nature had one more special treat to share with us. Suddenly, a buzzing hum broke the quiet. Looking in the direction of the sound, we saw a ruby-throated hummingbird feeding among the blue flag iris.

Later, on our leisurely drive back to town, Judy and I reviewed the colorful sights we had witnessed. Our gentle paddle on the magic bog lake had been calm and beautiful—an idyllic afternoon set apart from life's more blustery days.

Over the 15 years it took to find and paddle all 1,007 lakes in Itasca County, I experienced winds of countless different tempers. Many times powerful, wild gusts tossed the kayak and me around and blew us off course. Only once did that cause a real problem—the day Mother Nature captured my full

A female ruby-throated hummingbird visits
a blue flag iris along the shore of Mead Lake.

attention by flipping me into Steel Lake.

There were other winds as well—tumultuous emotional squalls that blew through my heart and sent me tumbling. Always, with time and the help of God and friends, I was able to find my way out of difficulty. More often than not, turbulent times pointed me in more favorable directions and prompted new ways of thinking. Life's refreshing breezes persuaded me to be courageous and to plunge ahead on paths I had not considered exploring, either in the woods or in my personal life.

During my kayaking quest, I learned to not fight against the wind, the water, the cold, or the heat. When an endeavor becomes a battle, Mother Nature always wins. It is best, I found, to simply mind my manners when on her turf.

Additional lessons learned related to a need to be more strategic in my thinking, planning, and equipment selection—especially as I moved toward paddling lakes that were difficult to reach.

Throughout the years, I carried a camera so that I could take photographs of interesting things I encountered. Early on, I used a five and a half pound 35 mm camera with an adjustable lens that allowed me to capture images at a distance or close up. Unfortunately, lugging it around also made my neck ache. Thanks to Horsethief Harry, I eventually advanced to the digital age. Now I use a six-megapixel gem that takes amazingly clear photographs.

Another lesson related to using maps. Over time, I accumulated 64 topographic maps, *The Itasca County Land Atlas and Plat Book*, county maps, and *The Northeastern Minnesota All Outdoors Atlas*—just to gain a comprehensive picture of Itasca County and the surrounding area. It took years for me to internalize the concept that inches on a flat page may translate into steep hills and distances of miles. Sometimes I thought the maps were wrong. Other times I chose to ignore topographic details, wetlands, or anything else that looked like an obstacle. Eventually, I respected the maps enough to realize that the shortest route to a lake might not be the easiest or quickest way to get there. I came to the conclusion that my maps were right at least 99 percent of the time.

Getting into lakes was one problem. Finding my way out again was another. I learned to carry pink ribbons in my pockets (bringing more than I thought I would need) and tied them to branches to mark my path. Kim the Kayaker taught me a Girl Scout trick that was worth its weight in Peanut Butter Patty cookies. She suggested that I turn around from time to time when I was walking in the woods so that I could see what the return trail would look like. I learned to keep track of landmarks too—a broken birch tree, a tall lone pine, or a raspberry patch. And eventually, I ended up adding a Global Positioning

System (GPS) to my collection of essential equipment.

Experience taught me that medical matters matter. One summer I figured I would get ahead of the game, so I stocked the red pony with plastic bottles I had filled with water. I reasoned that having a stash of water would save time and effort in the long run. After having diarrhea from April through August, however, I realized that it was worthwhile to be sure I had fresh water each time I left the house.

An additional health-related lesson came about in an uncomfortable way. One morning in early May I could find no largeleaf aster leaves or maple leaves, so I reached for birch bark after squatting in the woods. Immediately, it felt as if my bottom was on fire, and the burning continued until I arrived home and was able to shower. Now, I always keep toilet paper in the truck.

Along with the lessons learned about coping well on the water and in the woods, I also discovered some important things about myself.

Before I began the kayaking project, I was accustomed to letting others think for me, but in time I began to trust my own ability to make decisions and plans. I found that I am strong, capable, and able to do things on my own. While my divorce was the most emotionally expensive experience of my life, I survived. Over the years I have moved from always wanting to be with people to finding contentment in being by myself.

Now that the adventure is complete, people ask, "What are you going to do next?"

I answer, "God will provide something."

Even after paddling all of the lakes, I continue to gain energy from exploring and kayaking, so—with or without company—I will return to my favorite 50 lakes to savor their beauty and the joy of being on the water.

Exploring the wilds of Itasca County and meeting its people has been more satisfying and more fun than I could have imagined, but the opportunity for personal growth was the greatest gift I received from this incredible journey. And regarding the future, I know the winds of change will blow in something wonderful.

 remer Lake

On this misty October morning I am paddling the shoreline, recording sights and smells in the recesses of my mind to call upon in the coming hard-water days. Gently placing my paddle across the open cockpit so I may glide along and soak in the silent beauty of this scenic spot, I hear the peeping and squeaking conversation of beavers in their lodge just off my right shoulder. I can hardly believe my ears, or luck, to be in the secret world of these Kremer Lake residents. "What a gift," I think to myself. I am learning to keep my mouth shut and my ears and eyes wide open.

Epilogue

The Kayak Lady

In my head, the Kayak Lady and Mary Shideler are two very different people. Mary is the responsible one who foots the bills and cleans up after that rowdy, energetic, I-will-do-what-I-want-when-I-want-to-girl, the Kayak Lady. The Kayak Lady is strong, fearless, always on the edge. She gets away with damn near anything. Mary is becoming more of an introvert as the clock ticks. The Kayak Lady also loves the quiet, alone times, but with three shakes of a lamb's tail she becomes quite an extrovert. Both love brownies. The two of them sleep together and eat together. Mary wishes the Kayak Lady would show up and do more around the red house than load the kayak, use the phone and washroom, and grab fresh water bottles and a few apples. The Kayak Lady better start earning an income soon, or Mary will throw her out!

ise Old Owl

Carrying the kayak downhill, I inhale the sweet smell of conifers. Rounding a bend I catch a glimpse of an enormous white pine at the water's edge. Loons call out. As I set the boat in the water, I see the pair join together near the middle of 48-acre Willeys Lake. Later, I see their nest along the boggy shoreline. This is perfect: one old cabin, no boats, no people. The bog rosemary is blooming, and cedar trees stand watch over all. Although it is midday, an owl hoots from somewhere across the water. Someone told me an owl will hoot just before it rains. It sure looks like rain. Rain or shine, I am here and keen to paddle.

Acknowledgments

I am grateful to the following sponsors for their contributions:

• Bending Branches sent a Tail Wind kayak paddle.

• Buchanan Paddles gave me a custom-made Greenland-style kayak paddle.

• Pygmy Boats, Inc. supplied me with an Osprey 13 kayak.

• Spring Creek Outfitters, Inc. furnished a sturdy kayak cart with 16-inch wheels.

• Sterns, Inc. provided me with an inflatable personal floatation device.

Thank you to the following photographers for the use of their images:

Harry Johnson — pages ix, 5, 14, 87, 134, and 141
Catherine McLynn — pages 68 and 71
Derek Montgomery — pages iii, 84, and covers
All other photos were taken by Mary Shideler.